THE ILLUSTRATED FAMILY

ENCYCLOPEDIA

OF THE

LIVING BIBLE

THE ILLUSTRATED FAMILY
ENCYCLOPEDIA
OF THE
LIVING BIBLE

SAN FRANCISCO PRODUCTIONS, INC.

CHICAGO

536

SPECIAL CONSULTANTS AND CONTRIBUTORS

CHARLES F. KRAFT, Ph.D.
Professor of Old Testament Interpretation
Garrett Biblical Institute
Evanston, Illinois

EDWARD P. BLAIR, Ph.D.
Harry R. Kendall Professor of
New Testament Interpretation
Garrett Biblical Institute
Evanston, Illinois

JOHN L. McKENZIE, S.J.
Professor of Theology
University of Notre Dame
Notre Dame, Indiana

HERBERT C. BRICHTO
Professor of Bible
Hebrew Union College–Jewish Religious Institution
Cincinnati, Ohio

ALLEN PAUL WIKGREN
Chairman, Department of New Testament
Language and Early
Christian Literature
University of Chicago,
Chicago, Illinois

VOLUME 14

EPISTLES-REVELATION

AND

THE FAMILY BIBLE
REFERENCE
SECTION

· W - X - Y - Z ·

EPISTLES
REVELATION

☐ Twenty-one books of the New Testament have the form of letters. They may be divided into two classes: those attributed to Paul and those ascribed to other early Christian writers. They are addressed to individual churches, groups of churches, or the whole church, to assist the readers with specific problems of belief and conduct, to strengthen their faith and fidelity, and to inform them of the circumstances of the writers. Five have individual persons as addressees (I, II Timothy, Titus, Philemon, III John), but the character of their contents indicates that most of them were intended to be read in the churches with which the individuals were associated.

☐ Not all of the letters attributed to Paul may have been composed by him. The vocabulary, style, and theology of some (II Thessalonians, Ephesians, Colossians, I and II Timothy, Titus) have led certain scholars to question the traditional ascription, but other scholars have defended all of them as Paul's. The Epistle to the Hebrews, traditionally connected with Paul, makes no claim in its text to Pauline authorship and is quite certainly by another writer. If some letters were composed in Paul's name by friends and disciples, they nonetheless bear witness to his mind and spirit, inasmuch as disciples usually reflect the outlook of their mentors.

☐ Paul's letters, for the most part, were written in the course of a busy missionary career. Sometimes his authority as a Christian apostle was under attack and he was forced to defend himself (Galatians, II Corinthians). Persecution of his converts threatened to unnerve them and turn them away from their new faith (I Thessalonians, Philippians). Pagan beliefs and practices began to corrupt the purity of church life (I Corinthians). False teachers undertook to undo his work (Galatians, II Thessalonians, Colossians). His projected visit to Rome led him to seek to counter opposition there and arouse that church's support of his anticipated missionary venture in Spain (Romans). In prison he wished to thank his favorite church for a gift sent to him (Philippians). He pleaded for a runaway slave who had become a Christian brother (Philemon). His letters are not to be viewed as theological treatises addressed to a general public; they are personal missives to specific Christian readers, mostly children in the faith, whom he wishes to help with their problems and whose spirit of brotherhood he wishes to cultivate.

☐ The letters by other Christian leaders have generally a less specific character than most of Paul's. They are addressed, for the most part, to groups of churches or to the church in general and deal with universal Christian problems: actual or threatened apostasy to Judaism or pagan religion (Hebrews); Christian attitudes and conduct in time of persecution (I Peter); the need for a strong ethical element in Christian faith and life (James); the rise of heresy in the church (I, II John, Jude, II Peter); insubordination of a church leader (III John).

☐ The book of Revelation comes fittingly at the end of the Bible, for it describes the completion of God's purpose in the creation and redemption of the world. This purpose is shown to embrace the destruction of all evil and the coming of the Kingdom of God as the reward of the righteous. In this book Jesus Christ is represented as the instrument through whom God's purpose is both revealed and executed.

☐ Revelation was written by a leader of the church in Asia Minor who had been exiled to the island of Patmos in a time of bitter persecution of the church, probably by the emperor Domitian and his confederates in A.D. 95. All subjects in the empire seem to have been required to recognize the emperor's deity, perhaps by burning incense before his image. Those who refused were executed, banished, or deprived of their property. By the time of the writing of Revelation many Christians had paid the bitter price of refusal (2:13; 6:9). The whole church was in danger of succumbing and losing the right to admission to the Kingdom of God, which the writer believed was coming soon. He therefore undertook to warn the church and stimulate fidelity to the true God and his Son, Jesus Christ.

☐ The message is given in highly symbolic language, conventional among the Jews in such literature. It served to conceal the meaning of the book from the persecutors while allowing full flight to the imagination of the writer and the readers. Some truths can be communicated only by the use of metaphor and symbol. "Earth has no net of language in which to snare the skies." In arresting symbols, often puzzling to the modern reader, the book declares that God is the Lord of history, that human destiny is in his hands, and that good will outlast evil. Therefore, the righteous can go on being righteous in the knowledge that victory will at last be theirs.

—Edward P. Blair

8

PAUL, a servant of JESUS
CHRIST, called to be an apostle,
separated unto the gospel of
God.   (Rom. 1 : 1)

The Gospels, giving an account of the life, teaching and death of Jesus, are followed by the Acts of the Apostles,
which continue the story of the early days of Christianity till the arrival of St. Paul at Rome. The Acts are followed by the Epistles, twenty-one in number, ten or perhaps thirteen of which were written by St. Paul. The
series opens with the epistle to the Romans, setting out the doctrine of God's wrath against unrighteousness, the
wrongs done by both Jews and Gentiles, the Christian doctrine of salvation, and an exhortation to a life of
righteousness, the performance of civil and social duties, charity and unity. Though placed first in the list of
St. Paul's letters, Romans is by no means the first chronologically; the New Testament arrangement of them is
roughly in descending order of length. Romans is unique in the Pauline canon in that it was written to a church
neither founded nor yet visited by the Apostle, probably from Corinth in about A.D. 56. The illustration is
taken from a codex of the Pauline epistles of the third century A.D., fragments of which were found in 1930;
it shows Romans 8 : 15-25.

I AM debtor both to the Greeks, and to the Barbarians . . .   (Rom. 1 : 14)

The apostle includes here within the scope of his teaching the two groups then constituting the civilized world. The term "Greeks" as used in this context is not confined to the Greek or Hellenic nation, which evolved the Greek culture and then spread it across the world in the Hellenistic period, till it was adopted by Rome. One of the factors which aided this spread of Hellenism was the absence of any racial or religious discrimination in the Hellenistic world; a man was measured only by the degree of his adoption of Hellenic culture (see V.12:89). St. Paul himself was to a great extent an inheritor of the Greek tradition, as were most of the Jews living in the Diaspora. The growth of Christianity was already helped by the uniform culture, including language and literature, thus created by the Hellenistic world. At the same time, many peoples of antiquity — and above all the Jews — became increasingly conscious of their own traditions as opposed to those of Hellenism; although classed as "barbarians" (originally meaning "people of uncouth tongue", as opposed to the mellifluous Greek), they were no less important for the spread of Christianity. As a Hellenized Jew, St. Paul declares himself a debtor to both types of culture then prevalent.

Reproduced, on the left, is a typical Greek from the Mausoleum of Halicarnassos, 4th cent. B.C.; and, on the right, the bronze head of a Cyrenian barbarian, fashioned by a Greek artist in the first century A.D.

AN instructor of the foolish,
a teacher of babes . . .

(Rom. 2 : 20)

In the complex world of Hellenistic culture, a man's education counted more than any other factor in his social standing. It was therefore extremely important to go to the right teachers from the beginning. The rich could engage a special slave, called a pedagogue (lit. "leader of children") to take care of the education of their offspring. Such a teacher is portrayed on the Greek vase of the fifth century B.C., reproduced above. He is an oldish, balding man, with a thick beard; the laurel wreath on his brow indicates his dedication to Apollo, the god of poetry. His stick is leant against his chair. He is holding his left hand behind his back, while instructing his (invisible) pupils with his right, in which he is holding a stylus (writing stick). It is quite likely that St. Paul is here referring to a Jewish teacher of "babes" or small children; for in the days of the Hasmonaeans, Rabbi Simon ben Shetah had decreed universal instruction in reading and writing, and illiteracy thereafter became rare among the Jews. After completing their elementary education, more advanced pupils were entrusted to the schooling of a teacher of rhetoric (which then included literature and the art of expressing oneself in writing and speech). The illustration below, taken from a tomb relief of the third cent. A.D. found in Germany, shows a teacher (bearded, seated on the cathedra – see V.12:63) in the centre, with a seated student holding a roll on either side of him. A third student is just seen arriving on the right.

BEING justified freely by his grace through the redemption that is in CHRIST JESUS.   (Rom. 3 : 24)

The original meaning of the Greek word translated "redemption" in this verse (*apolytrosis*) is the emancipation of a slave. Although the institution of slavery is recognised both in the Old and New Testaments, as it was in the whole of the ancient world, yet all ancient religions as well as systems of law conceded that, just as a free man could become enslaved, so a slave could regain his freedom. Jewish law did not allow the enslavement of a Hebrew to continue beyond the sabbatical year (Ex. 21 : 2-6). In Greek religion the setting free of a slave was a pious act, as is shown by the many inscriptions at Delphi commemorating such emancipations. Roman law too admitted the freeing of a slave, either by payment of a sum of money or by the last will and testament of his master. Certain ceremonies had to be performed to make the freeing of a slave valid; they are portrayed on the relief shown in the illustration from the first century A.D., in which two slaves are being freed. One of them, already a free man, shakes the hand of his former owner; the other is kneeling to be touched by the magistrate's rod (*vindicta*) as a sign of his manumission. Both are wearing the high cap called *pileus*, the cap worn by freemen.

FOR the scripture saith unto Pharaoh, Even for this same purpose have I raised thee up, that I might show my power in thee . . . (Rom. 9 : 17)

The great miracle at the beginning of the history of Israel, the Exodus, and in particular the passage of the Red Sea and the destruction of Pharaoh and his host, has left an indelible impression on the consciousness of the Jewish people down the ages. It is referred to again and again in the prophetic and poetical literature of the Old Testament (Neh. 9 : 11; Ps. 135 : 9; Ps. 136 : 15 etc.) and occupies a prominent position in the frescoes of the synagogue of Dura Europus. As an outstanding example of the salvation effected by God's grace it figures in the prayers, both Jewish and Christian, which list this kind of miracle. As such it is also represented in early Christian art. The example shown here is a mosaic panel in the church of Santa Maria Maggiore in Rome, now attributed to the time of Pope Sixtus III (432-440), but based on earlier Jewish representations originating in Judaeo-Greek circles at Alexandria. The scene depicts, on the right, the "City of Egypt", with Pharaoh's forces issuing from it and precipitating themselves into the Red Sea. On the left Moses, with his miraculous rod, is parting the waters, with the Israelites behind him. Pharaoh, represented as an old man with white beard and hair, is drowning in the sea, still clad in the purple of royalty and with his shield held high, as if to protect himself from the wrath of Heaven.

HATH not the potter power over the clay, of the same lump to make one vessel unto honour and another unto dishonour?   (Rom. 9 : 21)

The craft of pottery is one of the oldest of the manual occupations of mankind; it reaches back at least to the Neolithic period. The ancients regarded the making of a vessel as an act of creation not unlike that by which God created the world, and regarded the helplessness and absolute dependence of the clay in the hand of the potter as a figure of the relation between the Almighty and His creatures. We find this type of simile in the utterances of the prophet Isaiah (Isa. 29 : 16) and the prophet of the deliverance (Isa. 45 : 9; 64 : 8), as well as in the sayings of Jeremiah (18 : 6 — see Vol. 7, p. 30 for ancient representations of the potter). Here St. Paul employs the same simile to illustrate his teaching of the election of some to Divine grace and the rejection of others, just as the potter determines the various uses to which his vessels shall be put. The illustration, from an ancient relief of the Roman period, shows a potter working on his wheel and attaching a handle to a vessel. The wheel used then was of the same shape and construction as those of the earlier period; but the clay was usually much better prepared and the ovens heated to a higher temperature, thus ensuring the production of finer vessels.

ＡND if some of the branches be broken off, and thou, being a wild olive tree, wert graffed in among them, and with them partakest of the root and fatness of the olive tree.   (Rom. 11 : 17)

The simile here employed by St. Paul is somewhat remarkable in being contrary to the usual practice of tree-grafting. The general rule is that a branch of a cultivated variety of tree is grafted on to a robust, wild variety, thus improving the latter's fruit. The city-born and city-bred St. Paul was not, it is true, as conversant as Jesus had been with the ways of the cultivator of the soil; but even so, he would hardly have made such a mistake as that attributed to him here, and have presumed that a wild olive was grafted on to a cultivated one. We must, on the contrary, assume that he used this exceptional case deliberately, in order to stress the uniqueness of the event he was discussing, namely the mystery of the rejection of the new religion by the people of God, the elected nation of Israel. The illustration shows some of the olive trees recently transplanted in Jerusalem, with grafts beginning to put forth small and as yet insignificant leaves.

FOR it has pleased them of Macedonia and Achaia to make a certain contribution for the poor saints which are at Jerusalem.
(Rom. 15 : 26)

Both the early Christian and the Jewish faiths centered on a group of people living in the Holy Land, but too poor to support themselves. It was therefore regarded as the duty of their co-religionists living in the Dispersion (Diaspora) to supply their needs, as befitted those believers who lived in comparative affluence, but in alien lands on a lower spiritual level than the focal area of their faith. With the rejection of the Jewish Law, Christianity in fact detached itself from the belief in the exclusive holiness of the country where it had originated. Yet enough of the old sentiment still remained for St. Paul to arrange for the needs of the Jerusalem Christian community, which in his time was small and living in hostile surroundings. Collections for the "saints" in Jerusalem, are referred to here and in 1 Cor. 16 : 1, where they are called *logia*. Exactly the same term is used in the ostracon shown below and dated to the 4th August, A.D. 63. In it a certain Psenamunis, the son of Pekysis, acknowledges the receipt of 4 drachmae, 1 obolus, as a contribution *(logia)* to the worship of Isis, the Egyptian goddess. It will be seen from this example that the type of collection mentioned in this verse was a common practice in antiquity.

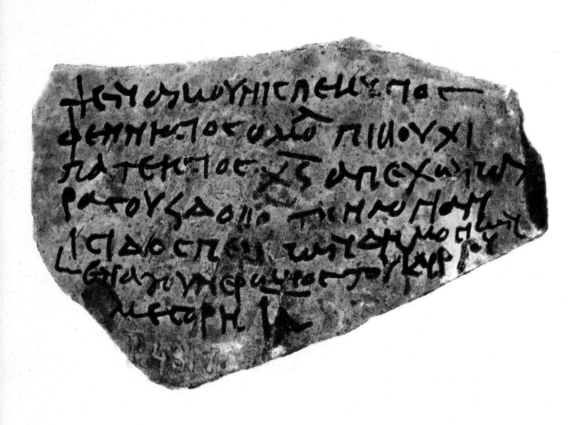

P<small>AUL</small>, called to be an apostle of J<small>ESUS</small> C<small>HRIST</small> through the will of God, and Sosthenes our brother, Unto the church of God which is at Corinth . . .   (1 Cor. 1 : 1-2)

The prominence of Corinth as a commercial centre and capital of the province of Achaia, and the comparatively long time that St. Paul laboured in the city (see V.13:89), gave the Christian community established there a special importance. In the course of his missionary activity, St. Paul wrote no less than four letters to the Corinthians, two of which have been included in the canon of the New Testament; when difficulties arose in this community he addressed to it some of his most important pronouncements. The first letter to the Corinthians was apparently written in A.D. 54 from Ephesus, where St. Paul stayed for several years (see V.13:91). This letter deals, first, with the divisions in the church at Corinth, leading to rivalry among the various parties and to an attempt to undermine his own prestige; with problems of sex, morality and marriage (especially pertinent in a city of light morals, as was Corinth in antiquity); with matters of contact with heathen society; and especially with the Apostle's well known views as "to the more excellent way" and the resurrection from the dead.
The photograph above shows the site of modern Corinth, with the Gulf of Corinth in the background and the mountains of Central Greece rising beyond it.

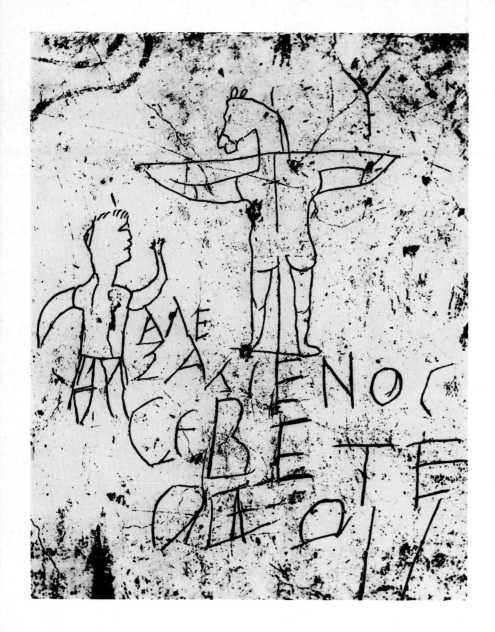

The main doctrine of Christianity, that the Son of God appeared in history as the man Jesus Christ, suffered death on the cross and thereby became the means of the salvation of mankind, was unacceptable to the two great groups with which it came into conflict. To the Jews such claims were indeed "a stumbling-block" (St. Paul's term). The Gentiles, it is true, were more used to the concept of incarnation, through contact with mystery religions, and the idea of gods appearing on earth. But their deities were triumphant gods; the idea of God suffering the ignominious death of a convicted felon must have seemed utter nonsense to the pagan mind. Statements to that effect are not lacking in the pagan polemics against Christianity, as far as they have been preserved in the writing of the Church Fathers. A graphic illustration of the hatred and contempt sometimes evoked by the Christian faith was found in 1856 in one of the guardrooms of the Palatine in Rome, the site of the imperial palace. It is a crude graffitto scratched on the wall in the first half of the third century A.D. and shows a man kneeling to a crucified figure with an ass's head; the inscription states that there is "Alexamenos worshipping his god". The allusion to Christianity is evident; similar calumnies regarding the worship of an ass had already been uttered by the enemies of the Jews in the Hellenistic period.

Y̶ET not the wisdom of this world, nor of the princes of this world, that come to nought.
(1 Cor. 2 : 6)

In the time of St. Paul, humanity was quite clearly divided into the governing and the governed. With the subjugation of the whole Mediterranean world by the Romans, most of the peoples of this area lost control of their destinies. Even in Rome itself, the common people had, after the establishment of the empire, no more say in the ruling of the world nominally ruled by them; politics were now a matter for the Roman aristocracy which governed in the name of an all-powerful emperor. The "princes" (lit. *archontes* — "rulers") of the world were the governors and commanders appointed by him. Although the Epistles here advocate the acceptance of their authority (see p. 49), St. Paul was nevertheless well aware of the transient nature of their power as compared with the eternity envisaged in his religious teaching. The illustration above shows what was probably the central group of those ruling the world at this time — a procession of senators and members of the imperial family on their way to do sacrifice. It was found on the frieze of the *Ara Pacis* ("Altar of Peace") erected by Augustus in Rome on his triumphal return after the pacification of Gaul and Spain, in 13 B.C. It gives a clear idea of the haughty, yet public-spirited, character of this ruling aristocracy of St. Paul's time.

Aaccording to the grace of God which is given unto me, as a wise master-builder, I have laid the foundation, and another buildeth thereon . . . (1 Cor. 3 : 10)

As a citizen of "no mean city"(seeV.13:97)and a great traveller all over the eastern part of the Roman Empire, St. Paul was familiar with the immense building activity which was going on throughout the Roman world in the first decades of the empire. As soon as the civil wars which had troubled Rome in the first century B.C. ended with the establishment of the rule of Augustus (seeV.13:12), increasing prosperity in Rome and the provinces led to a wave of constructional works. Augustus himself boasted that he had found Rome a city of brick and had left it a city of marble ; and building on a similar scale went on everywhere in his time. In his simile St. Paul compares himself to a wise master-builder who laid the foundations of an edifice, while others completed the walls. With the increase of building activity the actual work of construction naturally became specialized and was divided among various contractors and workmen, one laying the foundations, another erecting the wall, a third adding the ornament. The illustration shows the building of the walls of Rome ; it was found on a relief in the Roman forum, dating to the first century A.D.

W HAT will ye? shall I come unto you with a rod ...   (1 Cor. 4 : 21)

The use of the rod to enforce judgments, and in general to uphold the authority of magistrates and courts, was common in antiquity. The Mosaic Law had on several occasions (e.g. Deut. 25 : 3) prescribed the use of stripes; and St. Paul himself (2 Cor. 11 : 24) had undergone the punishment thus prescribed. The Roman magistrates also relied on the use of the rod to punish anyone who opposed their authority; indeed the rods carried by the lictors were the symbol of their power (see the illustration, a relief from the time of the Early Empire, found at Portogruaro near Venice). The lictors, who were usually freedmen, carried bundles of rods, called *fasces*. In Rome, where the magistrate's power of sentencing to death was limited by the right of appeal to the people, they carried the rods only (as on the relief shown here); but in the provinces where the governors wielded absolute power of life and death, they had axes attached to the fasces. The number of lictors varied in accordance with the rank of the magistrate: praetors had six, consuls twelve and the emperor twenty-four. They walked in solemn procession in front of the magistrate, whenever he went about his official duties. In this verse St. Paul offers the Corinthians the alternative of being treated by him as an apostle or as a Roman magistrate.

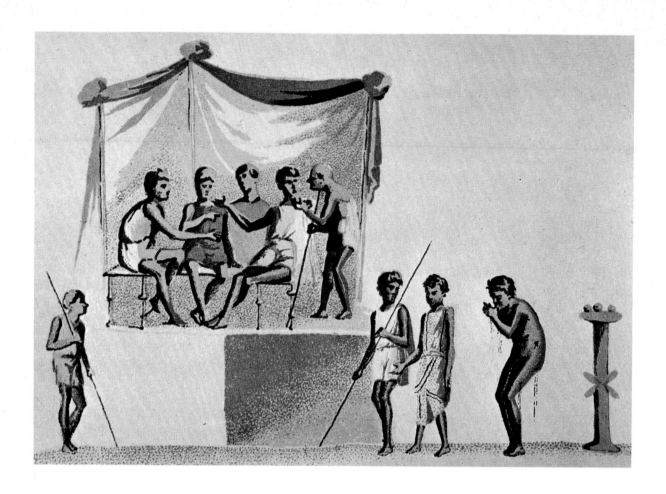

DARE any of you, having a matter against another, go to
law before the unjust, and not before the saints?

(1 Cor. 6 : 1)

Although the standard of justice in the Roman courts had improved under the empire in comparison with the
unsettled times of the late republic, the various religious communities, such as the Jews, nevertheless preferred
to settle disputes between their own members before their own tribunals, instead of having recourse to the
Roman authorities. Only in the case of outsiders or outcasts, such as St. Paul appeared to be in the eyes of the
leaders of the organized Jewish communities in the Diaspora, did their opponents appeal to the Romans or the
city rulers (see V. 13:84 and 90). How a Roman tribunal functioned we can see from the illustration above
which is a detail from a fresco found in the dyers'·quarter (the *Fullonica*) in Pompeii. The whole fresco depicts
a festivity of the dyers' guild, followed by disputes which end·in a fight. Those accused of disturbing the public
peace are brought before the magistrate who is represented sitting on his tribunal in informal dress (he is wearing
a tunic and not a toga) and flanked by his assessors (see p. 57). Witnesses are brought before him, while the
court-usher hands in two more of the disputants, one of whom is bleeding freely.

MEATS for the belly, and the belly for meats . . .　　(1 Cor. 6 : 13)

The fundamental materialism of the Roman mind found its most grotesque expression in the prosperous times of the Early Empire in a spread of gluttony unparalleled in history before or since. Latin literature abounds in descriptions of the gargantuan and ingeniously devised repasts eaten by wealthy Romans, from Lucullus, whose name became proverbial, to the emperor Vitellius, whose bloated countenance and many chins betray the nature of his favourite vice. A typical Roman meal, and a relatively simple one at that, is represented on the border of a mosaic found at Antioch and reproduced here. It dates to the third century A.D. The meal begins with eggs (hence the Roman saying "*ab ovo*" — lit. "from the egg", meaning from the beginning) and continues from right to left by way of a course of fish, ham and poultry, to its conclusion in the shape of a rich cake. Multiplied tenfold this would serve to give an idea of the récherché gastronomical titillations indulged in by many of the highest circles of the Gentile world, from which St. Paul draws his warning simile.

LET every man have his own wife, and let every woman have her own husband.

(1 Cor. 7 : 2)

In this verse St. Paul is proclaiming the Christian doctrine of marriage as opposed to the laxer morality of the pagan world, a subject on which the Roman satirical poets furnish us with only too much information. Yet there is as much contrary evidence to show that among the Greeks and Romans, especially in the middle and lower classes, conjugal ties were much respected and the standard of morality was high. The main proof of this is supplied by gravestones, with their inscriptions in which husbands or wives praise the virtues of the departed spouse. One such example is reproduced above; it is the tombstone, found at Rome, of one Aurelius Hermia, a butcher from the Viminal hill, and his wife Aurelia Philemation. The husband and wife are represented in the centre clasping hands affectionately. The accompanying inscription serves to emphasize the union of their spirits; in it the husband praises the virtues of his wife "the chaste, modest, faithful to her husband", while the wife speaks highly of her "loving husband and fellow-freedman, who was more than a father to her". Such examples could be multiplied to show that all was not rotten in the Roman world in the first century A.D.

·

FOR though there be that are called gods, whether in heaven or in earth, (as there be gods many and lords many)... (1 Cor. 8 : 5)

In ancient religions the boundaries between gods and men were not drawn as strictly as in the monotheistic faiths which superseded them. Gods descended from Olympus and mixed with men; great heroes were taken up to heaven and worshipped after their deaths as gods. If Heracles, who was a benefactor of humanity, became a god, why not Alexander the Great, whose deeds were at least as magnificent? The Hellenistic kings profited from this belief and established cults of themselves as "gods manifest" (*epiphanoi*); the cases of Antiochus IV of Syria and of the Ptolemies, kings of Egypt, are especially well documented. Such deification of a living Greek ruler was supposed to have a great effect on his Oriental subjects who were used to regarding their dynasts as gods. The Roman emperors were usually deified only after their deaths, following the example of Julius Caesar; and Augustus discouraged worship of himself, if unaccompanied by that of the goddess Roma (see p. 96). Gaius Caligula, on the other hand, firmly believed himself a god and acted accordingly; and even his more reasonable successor, Claudius, was worshipped in his lifetime in the provinces. St. Paul was therefore alluding to a well-known practice of the Gentile world when he mentioned the gods in heaven and on earth. The illustrations show, for comparison, a representation of Jupiter, the principal deity of the Roman pantheon, on a Pompeian painting, with his sceptre and the eagle at his feet, and a statue of the emperor Claudius as a god, with the same attributes.

WHO goeth a warfare any time at his own charges? who planteth a vineyard, and eateth not of the fruit thereof? or who feedeth a flock, and eateth not of the milk of the flock?

(1 Cor. 9 : 7)

Although the examples quoted in this verse refer to the limitations imposed on the Hebrew rulers in calling up the people for military service (Deut. 20 : 5-8), the underlying realities are those of the period in which St. Paul lived. Those familiar with Roman military and economic activities could easily supply the background of these similes for themselves. There was continuous warfare of some sort on one or another of the imperial frontiers; while agriculture (or rather viticulture, in the example chosen) and the rearing of flocks were common pursuits within those borders. The illustrations show two of the three occupations mentioned in the verse. In the relief above, the emperor Trajan (98-117) is seen starting for the Second Dacian War. The relief is part of the decoration of the column dedicated to this emperor at Rome. It shows the emperor standing in his ship and setting sail from a harbour, with a lantern shining in front of him and citizens holding lighted torches on the left above. The other relief, also found at Rome, shows the peaceful life of farmers and shepherds; a shepherd is milking the flock, while another above is cutting down a tree to make a hut. These idyllic scenes form a sharp contrast with the martial scene above them.

$\mathbf{K}$NOW ye not that they which run in a race run all, but one receiveth the prize? . . .
Now they do it to obtain a corruptible crown; but we an incorruptible. I therefore so run,
not as uncertainly; so fight I, not as one that beateth the air.   (1 Cor. 9 : 24-26)

St. Paul, although of Jewish origin and learned in the Law, was nevertheless a Roman citizen and a member
of a wealthy family living in a Hellenistic city. He was therefore thoroughly familiar with the Greek way of life
in which athletics played a most important part. Contests of skill in chariot-riding, racing on foot (see lower
picture) or on a horse, hurling the spear and the discus, wrestling and boxing, were held in all Greek cities and in
those cities of the Orient which had adopted Greek culture. Naturally, therefore, the apostle uses metaphors
drawn from the world of athletics to illustrate his case when addressing the Corinthians. He here refers to the
foot race and to the crowns obtained by those victorious in the contests. The illustration on the left illustrates part
of the tombstone, found at Athens, of one Nikokles the son of Aristokles, a Greek of the Roman period. No less
than sixteen crowns are represented on the whole monument, standing for as many victories in athletic contests,
including the Great Panathenaic, the Games at Delphi, the Isthmian Games at Corinth, besides many others.
"Beating the air" refers to the sport of boxing, which is illustrated above from another vase of the fifth century
B.C. Two men are seen boxing in the centre, with onlookers standing by to assist the boxers and to judge the
contest (upper picture on right).

ᴀɴᴅ did all drink the same spiritual drink . . .   (1 Cor. 10 : 4)

The miracle at Rephidim (as related in Exodus 17 : 1-7 and again in Numbers 20 : 7-13), when Moses smote the rock and water came out of it, made a profound impression on succeeding generations; it is referred to again in Deut. 8 : 15 as "water brought out of the flinty rock" (cf. Vol. 3, p. 35) and in the poetic and prophetic literature of the Old Testament. The symbolic interpretation of the event here adopted by St. Paul has remained one of the basic tenets of the Christian church. Hence we find Moses' smiting of the rock represented in the catacomb paintings more than any other scene from the Old Testament. In the example chosen for illustration above, we see Moses as a bearded figure striking the rock in front of him with his staff. Water is gushing from the rock and an Israelite is bending down to drink from the spring which appears in such a miraculous way in the desert. This scene is combined with another to the left: there we see Moses loosing his sandals, as ordered by God who is represented by a hand issuing from a cloud above. The painting was discovered in the Catacomb of St. Callixtus at Rome and is now assigned to the fourth century A.D.

As some of them also tempted, and were destroyed of serpents.

(1 Cor. 10 : 9)

In alluding to the people who tempted God and were destroyed by serpents, St. Paul is of course referring to the plague of serpents which punished the Israelites in the desert, as told in Numbers 21 : 5-9 (cf. Vol. 2, p. 105). There was also a similar event in Greco-Roman mythology, represented in the famous work of art illustrated above. Laocoon, a Trojan priest, incurred the wrath of Apollo who sent serpents to destroy the sinner and his two sons. This story was the subject of a Late Hellenistic sculptured group (ca. 50 B.C.) which was later set up in Nero's palace on the Esquiline where it was discovered in 1506, profoundly influencing the art of the Renaissance. The artist represented the father in the centre of the group struggling with the two serpents; the younger son on the left has already perished, while the elder on the right tries to free himself from the reptiles' coils. The choice of the psychological moment of agony and despair, and the technical excellence of the execution render this sculpture one of the most striking and characteristic examples of the emotional art of the period. The disaster which befell Laocoon was also interpreted symbolically as an evil augury of the coming fall of Troy. As St. Paul was in Rome when this sculpture was about to be set up in Nero's Palace, he might well have seen it.

Every man praying or prophesying, having his head covered, dishonoureth his head. But every woman that prayeth or prophesieth with her head uncovered dishonoureth her head; for that is even all one as if she were shaven.

(1 Cor. 11 : 4-5)

The apostle intends to make the ritual practices of the Christians as different as possible from those of both the Jews and the Gentiles. Thus, it was a common Jewish custom, and one shared with many of the oriental nations, to keep one's head covered as a sign of respect and reverence. As, of course, the greatest reverence was due to God, He had to be worshipped with the head covered. In the same way the Romans, who normally went about bare-headed, used to draw a fold of their voluminous mantle, the toga, over their head when praying or sacrificing. The statuette reproduced on the left, which dates to the early empire, shows a Roman performing a libation; he has lifted his right hand towards heaven and has his head covered (cf. also the procession of senators on the *Ara Pacis,* p. 21, where the principal personages have their heads covered). Women in the Greek world, on the contrary, sacrificed with their heads uncovered (see on the right the drawing of a fresco found on the Aventine hill at Rome). In demanding that women keep their heads covered while praying, St. Paul conforms with Jewish usage, in which the uncovering of the head of a married woman was regarded as improper in the highest degree; but for men to pray bare-headed was an innovation.

WHEN I was a child, I spoke as a child, I understood as a child, I thought as a child; but when I became a man, I put away childish things. For now we see through a glass, darkly . . .
(1 Cor. 13 : 11-12)

Classical Greek art followed an idealizing tendency which did not regard the immature as a fit subject for artistic representation; hence, if we wish to learn about the games played by Greek children, we have to turn to the material provided by the craftsmen who painted the Attic vases, or to the Hellenistic period in which interest in children awoke. The example chosen here to illustrate the words of the apostle is taken from a Late Roman sarcophagus (see above) which was certainly the coffin of some child. As usual, the deceased is represented in his happiness in the other world, following his avocations during life. In this relief, a group of boys and girls is shown playing various children's games. The next verse contains an allusion to the mirrors used by the ancients. The word translated "glass" *(eisoptron)* refers to the common bronze mirrors, which could be polished till they imperfectly reflected the features of those looking into them (see, left, the reproduction of such a bronze mirror in its unpolished state); no clear image could be obtained in mirrors till as late as the 14th century A.D. when glass backed with tinfoil began to be used.

A ND even things without life, giving sound, whether pipe or
harp, except they give a distinction in the sounds, how shall it
be known what is piped or harped? For if the trumpet give an
uncertain sound, who shall prepare himself to the battle?

(1 Cor. 14 : 7-8)

The two verses above (together with 1 Cor. 13 : 1) list the most common
musical instruments known in antiquity (cf. also Vol. 9, pp. 62–63). They
are here illustrated from three monuments. Above is a Pompeian mosaic,
probably the copy of an Alexandrian painting. It depicts a street scene with
strolling players. On the left a woman is playing the double pipe; in the
centre an actor is dancing, accompanying himself with cymbals held in his
hands (for a reference to the "tinkling cymbal" see 1 Cor. 13 : 1). The third
actor is beating a hand-drum. All three figures are masked. The illustration
on page 35 (left), reproducing a wall painting from a Roman villa of
the first century A.D., shows a woman harpist holding her instrument
and conversing with another woman holding a drum. In contrast to these
instruments, which were much played in civilian life, the use of the trumpet
was reserved for fighting. The Roman army employed several kinds of
trumpet, some straight and some curved, and similar instruments were used
in the gladiatorial contests. In the relief reproduced, right, we see fighting
gladiators, and opposite them a group of trumpeters blowing their long,
straight trumpets, the *salpinx* mentioned in the Greek original of our verse.

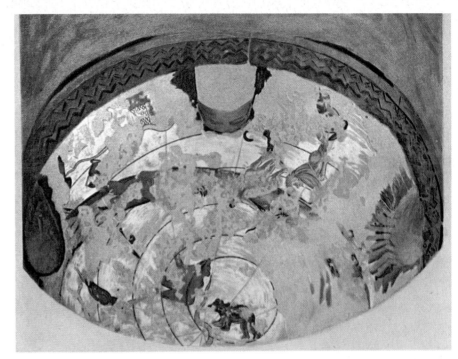

THERE are also celestial bodies and bodies terrestrial: but the glory of the celestial is one and the glory of the terrestrial is another. (1 Cor. 15 : 40)

Although both the Jewish and Christian religions rejected the astrological conception of the universe which was most common in the later centuries of antiquity (and which was officially adopted by the then prevailing Stoic philosophy), the conception of "celestial" and "terrestrial" bodies originating in it was nevertheless used in common parlance. The belief that the movement of the stars in heaven influenced the fate of men on earth has also left some traces in the Bible, as in the Song of Deborah (Judg. 5 : 20 — "the stars in their courses fought against Sisera"). It did not end with the end of the ancient world; horoscopes are found in later periods too, both in the Christian and in the Islamic world. The example shown here is a fresco from the Umaiyyad desert castle of Quseir 'Amra, in the wilderness beyond the Jordan, dating to the eighth century A.D. It shows the various constellations seen in the heavens at a certain date, and is painted on a dome in the palace which served as a hunting-lodge for the caliphs and was equipped with dining-rooms, a bath and other amenities.

Wᴿɪᴛᴛᴇɴ not with ink, but with the Spirit of the living God; not in tables of stone, but in fleshy tables of the heart.

(2 Cor. 3 : 3)

St. Paul contrasts the witness of the spirit with the various kinds of material record common in his time. Any kind of record for temporary use was made with a sharp pointed instrument on a tablet covered with wax; but this method of writing is not mentioned here. Writing of a more permanent character was done on papyrus or parchment with reed or bronze pens which had split nibs rather like their modern counterparts. The ink was kept in metal or faience ink-pots, with narrow openings or with covers to prevent the ink from spilling (see illustration on the right). Still more permanent in character was monumental writing on stone or bronze tablets. The ancients used to chisel out the dedications of both religious and civil buildings, as well as treaties, laws, and funerary inscriptions on monuments, on stone or metal tablets; as the metal tablets have mostly perished the writing on stone supplies the bulk of epigraphical information preserved. The specimen given here is a fragment of the Temple inscription (see V.13:96 for the whole text) found at Jerusalem, which forbade Gentiles to pass beyond a certain point in the Temple Court. It is a fairly good example of this kind of writing, with the guiding lines and the paint inside the letters still visible. When in Jerusalem, the apostle must have glanced at this inscription or at one of its copies.

As the serpent beguiled Eve . . .   (2 Cor. 11 : 3)

One of the fundamental tenets of the Christian religion is the belief that the Original Sin caused by Adam and Eve's fall in Paradise was redeemed by the sacrificial death of Jesus on the cross. We therefore find references to the Fall both in apostolic literature (as here and in Rom. 5 : 12-21; 1 Cor. 15 : 22, 45) and in early Christian art. These artistic representations of Adam, Eve and the serpent are probably derived from a cycle of pictures illustrating the biblical story which was evolved in the Hellenized Jewish circles at Alexandria, and has been preserved to some extent in the frescoes of the synagogue at Dura-Europus, the catacomb paintings, and illuminated Bible manuscripts. Adam and Eve are usually shown on either side of the tree, with the serpent winding round the trunk. The whole composition recalls the scenes illustrating the myth of the Argonauts, with Jason and Medea and the dragon serving as counterparts of Adam and Eve and the serpent. Another motif influencing this representation is the serpent guarding the golden apples of the Hesperides. Reproduced here is a fresco from the catacomb at Naples.

IN Damascus the governor under Aretas the king kept the city of the Damascenes with a garrison, desirous to apprehend me.   (2 Cor. 11 : 32)

St. Paul here gives a rather different version of the circumstances of his escape from Damascus from that in Acts 9 : 23-25 (see V.13:73-74). Instead of attributing his danger to the Jews, as stated by the author of the Acts, the apostle mentions that it was the governor of Damascus under king Aretas who tried to have him arrested. The Aretas referred to can, chronologically, only have been Harithath the Fourth, king of the Nabataeans, called Aretas in Greek; he ruled from 9 B.C. to A.D. 40. The Nabataeans were a people of Arab origin, who in the Persian period occupied Edom and the Negeb, developed the trade routes and agriculture around Petra, their capital, and in the arid areas under their control, as well as an art of no mean quality (see Vol. 8, pp. 50–51). They maintained themselves as vassals of Rome till A.D. 106, when they were subjected by Trajan and their country turned into a province named Arabia. While the dynasty lasted, it extended its sway over the desert east of the Jordan, and occasionally also ruled Damascus (once from 85-66 B.C. and again in the days of Caligula). It is to this latter period of their rule that St. Paul refers here. The interruption in the series of coins of the city of Damascus during this time (ca. A.D. 37-40) attests that the city was then not autonomous. The illustrations show a coin of Aretas with his portrait, on the left; and, on the right, an inscription in Nabataean found at Eboda ('Avdat) in the Negeb, bearing the names of Harithath and other Nabataean princes.

W HEREFORE take unto you the whole armour of God, that ye may be able to withstand in the evil day, and having done all, to stand. Stand therefore, having your loins girt about with truth, and having on the breastplate of righteousness; And your feet shod with the preparation of the gospel of peace. Above all, taking the shield of faith, wherewith ye shall be able to quench all the fiery darts of the wicked. And take the helmet of salvation, and the sword of the Spirit, which is the word of God. (Eph. 6 : 13-17)

The whole passage in verses 13-17 is based on reminiscences of Isaiah 59 : 17; but, naturally, in describing the "armour of God" St. Paul had before his eyes the type of defensive and offensive weapons which were common in the Greco-Roman world. The defensive part of the armour consisted of a helmet to protect the head, a breastplate to protect the chest (with a belt to keep it in place and to hold the sword), greaves to protect the legs, and a shield to ward off the blows of the enemy's sword and spear, and the darts from his bow (v. 16). The low penetrating power of ancient offensive weapons, which — except for the dreaded bow — depended on muscular power alone, made the use of armour worth while, even though it slowed down the movement of the soldier. In the period of the Roman empire the weight of the armour was gradually reduced till the revival of the armoured cavalry in the third century. In the illustration, taken from a vase painting by the Attic artist Duris (ca. 490 B.C.), we see Odysseus handing over to Neoptolemos the arms of his father Achilles. Although the vase is much earlier than St. Paul's epistle, the essential aspect of armour had not changed and we can see the various parts referred to in the above verses: the helmet, breastplate — made of metal scales — the shield, and the spear.

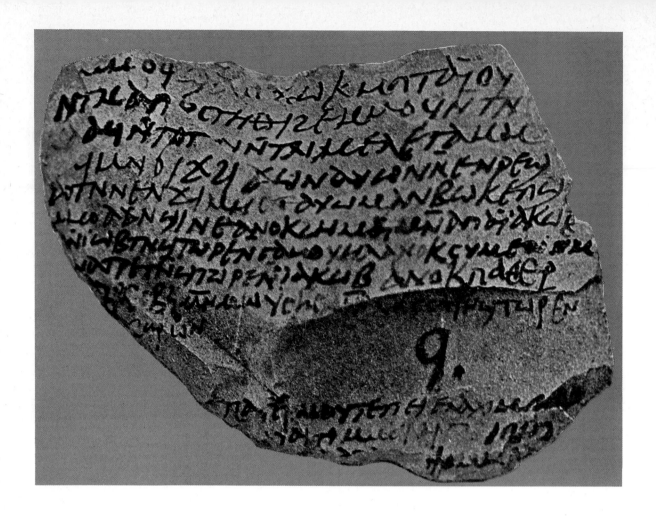

Paul and Timotheus, the servants of JESUS CHRIST, to all the saints in CHRIST JESUS which are at Philippi, with the bishops and deacons. (Phil. 1 : 1)

The early Christian Church, like all similar organizations, required the appointment of officials who could take charge of the common property of its members and administer it for the benefit of those entitled to help (Acts 6 : 1-6). These administrators were called *diakonoi* "servants"; their spiritual and moral qualifications are laid down in 1 Tim. 3 : 8. The "bishops" (Greek *episkopoi,* lit. "overseers") were appointed in the larger communities (Acts 20 : 17, 28) and were entrusted with the care of the faithful, like shepherds watching over their flocks. In the early days of Christianity the number of such overseers in one community was not limited to one, as in later times; at Philippi and at Ephesus there were several of them. An organization, however, was not contemplated at the outset, but developed gradually as the need for supervision of gatherings, regulation of conduct and a system of charitable relief required it. Women were not disqualified by their sex. All were expected to qualify for office by blamelessness of conduct and holiness of character. Office clearly meant service, and further implied prior discipline. The ostracon shown above, written in Egypt, ca. 600 A.D., sets forth the relations between bishops and deacons many centuries after St. Paul addressed the two groups in his letter to the Philippians. By then, it shows, candidates for the office of deacon pledged themselves to the organizational disciplines of the period.

ALL the saints salute you, chiefly they that are of Caesar's household.

(Phil. 4 : 22)

SALVIVS CAESAR
SER
SVPRA ARGENT

Roman aristocratic households comprised hundreds of slaves, some of whom laboured in the personal service of their master and others on his estates. In several cases slaves were even allowed to set up in a trade or craft, paying part of their profits to their owner. The imperial household was, from the time of Augustus to that of Trajan, organized on the aristocratic Roman model, but on a vastly larger scale. It contained thousands of slaves, some of whom, especially those who succeeded in obtaining their freedom, rose to the summit of political power. They in fact constituted the civil service of the early empire and, as such, wielded almost absolute powers in the emperor's name. In such a numerous community, many of whom came from Greece and the Orient, Christianity early found a foothold, especially because of its appeal to those of lowly social status (see also the next page). The Alexamenos whose devotion to Jesus was ridiculed in a caricature (p. 20) was also a member of the imperial household. Reproduced here is the bust of Salvius, a servant of the emperor Tiberius, who was in charge of the silver plate *(Salvius Caesari servus supra argentum)*; it was found in the Second Columbarium (cemetery) of the Vigna Codini on the Appian Way, near Rome.

WHERE there is neither Greek nor Jew, circumcision nor uncircumcision, Barbarian, Scythian, bond nor free . . .
(Col. 3 : 11)

The human appeal of Christianity, as taught by St. Paul, lay in its complete disregard of the social hierarchy of the early Roman empire. To the various communities of national or religious origin, each regarding the others with suspicion and occasionally with contempt, the apostle stresses their unity in the new faith. Greeks, who regarded the rest of the world as barbarians (see Vol. 13:109; 14:12). Jews, who drew a difference between those who had entered the covenant of Abraham and all others, barbarians who suffered from inferiority of status because of their lack of Greek culture, and even the uncouth Scythians, the most savage of barbarians — all could equally hope for redemption. So could even the slaves, who had lost their freedom in this world, but would participate in the salvation of Paradise. The manual tasks performed by slave labour are illustrated by a Roman relief, showing the placing of blocks on a sumptuous funeral monument in the shape of a temple (on the right); the work is carried out with the aid of a machine consisting of a high mast, with ropes attached to it by pulleys, the motive force being supplied by a treadmill (lower left) worked by the exertions of slaves. The relief comes from the tomb of the Haterii at Rome, from the first cent. A.D.

FOR I bear him record, that he hath a great zeal for you, and them that are in Laodicea, and them in Hierapolis. Luke, the beloved physician, and Demas, greet you.   (Col. 4 : 13-14)

At the end of his epistle to the Colossians, the inhabitants of a city in the upper part of the Lycus Valley in the province of Asia, St. Paul conveys the greetings of one of his disciples, Epaphras, a native of the city, and adds an appreciation of his zeal for the Christian communities at Colossae and the neighbouring cities of Laodicea and Hierapolis. The former was situated about twelve miles west of Colossae, and was probably founded by Antiochus II Theos (261-246 B.C.) and named in honour of his wife Laodice. It had a famous temple of the Phrygian god Men, with a medical school attached. It was also a centre of the wool trade and of banking. Hierapolis, now called Tambuk Kalessi, was situated north-west of Laodicea, between the Lycus and the Meander; it was famous for its hot springs which were used for baths, and for its temple of the goddess Kybele. It had a long main street (see view above) with colonnades on either side, and a gymnasium, temples and theatres. It is first mentioned c. 190 B.C. and was a flourishing city till an earthquake in A.D. 60. Luke the physician, mentioned here, is generally identified with the Evangelist and the companion of St. Paul on his voyages. The profession of physician was highly esteemed in the Greek and Roman world; some of its practitioners, especially the physicians of the emperor, were able to do great services to their native towns and were honoured by them (V.13:38). The illustration below is a reproduction of a Roman relief, the tombstone of a physician named Jason, who is seen auscultating a patient.

PAUL, and Silvanus, and Timotheus, unto the church
of the Thessalonians . . .   (1 Thess. 1 : 1)

Two of St. Paul's epistles are addressed to the community of Thessalonica (modern Saloniki), the great city on
the coast of Macedonia. Originally called Thermae, after the hot springs in its vicinity, it was renamed in 315 B.C.
by Cassander after his wife Thessalonike, the sister of Alexander the Great. The city prospered owing to its
position at the junction of the Egnatian way, the principal line of communications across the Balkans, and the
northwards route to the Danube, and also because of its magnificent harbour. Under the Romans it was the
capital of the Second province of Macedonia, and a free city from 42 B.C. onwards. In the time of St. Paul there
was a Jewish community there with its own synagogue (Acts 17 : 1-13). The church at Thessalonica was founded
by St. Paul on his second missionary journey. On being forced to leave the city, the apostle wrote from Athens,
after having received a report from Timothy as to the state of the community. The main doctrinal points of the
letter treat of the imminent return of Christ; the second epistle is presumably a later reiteration. The illustration is a
view of the city and its harbour on the Thermaic Gulf as it was called in antiquity, now the Gulf of Saloniki.
The view is taken from the heights surrounding the city and forming its principal line of defence.

THEREFORE let us not sleep, as do others; but let us watch and be sober.   (1 Thess. 5 : 6)

Among the exhortations with which St. Paul concludes his epistle to the Thessalonians is one to the faithful to watch vigilantly for the second coming of Jesus, the time of which was uncertain though the event itself was sure and would probably occur with dramatic suddenness. In the following verse (8) the faithful are adjured to put on "the breastplate of faith and for an helmet the hope of salvation". These military metaphors (for which compare p. 39 and Ephesians 6 : 14), as well as the exhortation to "keep watch and be sober", make it probable that the apostle here intended a comparison with the splendid discipline of the Roman army, with which he must have become familiar on his travels and in the course of his perils. It was owing to this unquestioning obedience to orders that the Romans were able to make good their defeats and to take full advantage of their victories. The vigilant alertness referred to is illustrated by the bronze statuette, about 9 in. high (on the right) of a Roman soldier in full armour. It shows the legionary with a crested helmet on his head, and a cuirass made of overlapping bands of metal which are fastened down in front, with a kilt of leather or metal strips underneath. He is also wearing trousers and shoes. The spear, sword and shield which completed the Roman soldier's equipment are missing here.

FOR we hear that there are some which walk among you disorderly, working not at all, but are busybodies.   (2 Thess. 3 : 11)

In referring to the "busybodies" who shun all work, the apostle most likely had in mind the parasite, a common figure in ancient Greek and especially Roman society. The term originally meant anyone "feeding with" *(parasitos)* someone else, such as the assistants of an official who helped him to collect taxes in kind; then those dining at the public expense; and, finally, anyone who succeeded in worming himself into the good graces of the rich and feeding at their tables. Such types were the standing butts of ancient satire. Their eternal hunger and their readiness to undergo any humiliation for the sake of food are in particular an inexhaustible source of jokes in Greek and Roman comedy. As the ancient actors appeared in masks, which indicated the type of person they were supposed to represent, the audience could at once distinguish the parasite. One such representation, from a Pompeian fresco, is shown here. We see, on the left, the paunchy and ever hungry parasite conversing with a courtesan and her servant and making a sign to avert the evil eye. All of the three are common characters in the comedy of manners, which was the standard type of entertainment in Hellenistic and early Roman times in the Greek world and thus quite familiar to an educated person like St. Paul.

THE salutation of Paul with mine own hand, which is the token in every epistle . . . (2 Thess. 3 : 17)

The art of writing, and especially of writing legibly, was much rarer in antiquity than to-day; therefore, anyone who could do so employed trained scribes to whom he dictated his letters. This was also the practice of St. Paul who, in another letter (Gal. 6 : 11), refers to the large letters written in his own hand. In order to assure the recipient that the letter was authentic, the sender usually added a note in his own hand, such as the word "Greeting", the date and the like. St. Paul authenticates his letters by adding a "salutation in his own hand", as did most of the letter writers whose letters have been preserved on papyrus. As an example of a letter indited in two hands we reproduce here a letter written on the 24th of August A.D. 66, on behalf of the peasant Harmyisis, to Papiscus, governor of Oxyrrhynchos. It is written in a clerkly hand, with additions in another cursive script.

N<small>EITHER</small> give heed to fables and endless genealogies . . .
(1 Tim. 1 : 4)

In his warning against false doctrine the writer refers to the "fables and endless genealogies" of the pagans. After a period in which Greek myths evolved spontaneously and freely, they were systematized by scholars and linked together by a genealogy of the gods, in which they were arranged in generations and related to each other by supposed family ties. Another prolific source of fables and genealogies was the desire of every Hellenized city — and for this purpose Rome could also be counted as one — to be connected in one way or another with a Greek god or hero as its founder. In Rome especially an elaborate line of descent was fabricated, and apparently also believed in. The founders of Rome, Romulus and Remus, were described as the sons of the god Mars and the Vestal Rhea Silvia; exposed in the Tiber, they were given suck by a she-wolf, till they were discovered by shepherds and brought up among them. The illustration shows this legend as represented on an altar found at Ostia: the she-wolf and the twins are seen below, protected by an eagle; the shepherds with their characteristic crooks are visible above them, while the god of the River Tiber watches over the twins in the lower right corner of the relief. The altar is dated by an inscription to 124 A.D.

PRAYERS ... be made for
all men ... for kings and for
all that are in authority ...
(1 Tim. 2 : 1-2)

The request made here to pray "for kings and all that are in authority" is the more astonishing if we remember that, at the time of the composition of this letter, A.D. 63-67, the Roman world was governed by Lucius Domitius Ahenobarbus, the son of Agrippina (the daughter of Germanicus and later on the second wife of Claudius the emperor) and C. Domitius Ahenobarbus, a Roman noble. After his adoption by the emperor Claudius, the young man was named Nero Claudius Drusus Germanicus Caesar; he ascended the throne in A.D. 54. After a period of five years during which his ministers governed well for him, Nero began a career of tyranny and debauch which rendered his name a byword. He removed the members of his family one by one and terrorized the aristocracy. His artistic aspirations to shine as poet and singer rendered him odious in the eyes of the serious-minded Romans. After the great fire in Rome, in 64 A.D., during which he appeared as a vocal artist commemorating the Fall of Troy, he directed popular suspicion away from himself as the arsonist and persecuted the Christians; St. Paul seems to have lost his life in this persecution. Finally, the armies in the provinces rose against the deranged emperor, and he perished in 68 by his own hand. Nevertheless, it was this worst emperor of the great apostle's lifetime that is singled out as one to be prayed for. Reproduced above is one of the many portraits of Nero, made at Rome.

I WILL therefore that men pray every where, lifting up holy hands, without wrath and doubting. In like manner also, that women adorn themselves in modest apparel, with shame-facedness and sobriety . . .

(1 Tim. 2 : 8-9)

The raising up of the hands to heaven was the common attitude of prayer in the East, as contrasted with the covering of the head and folding of the arms in the Roman form of supplication (see p. 32). In the paintings of the catacombs we find many representations of the early Christians praying with lifted hands. The reproduction above is a painting in the catacomb of St. Callixtus at Rome. In this scene we see a woman, dressed in long robes, with her head veiled, and without jewels or other ornaments such as are roundly condemned by the apostle in other epistles (see p. 63). The woman, on the left, is wearing the long tunic or *stola*, which was the principal female garment among the Romans; the tunic has long sleeves and is adorned solely by two broad stripes of colour. Over it she has in addition a mantle, the *palla*, of a darker colour. Her head is modestly veiled. On the right is a youth clad in a tunic, also lifting up his hands in prayer. Many similar representations have been found in other catacombs, indicating that the teaching of the apostle bore fruit among the Christians of Rome. It should, of course, be remembered that the early adherents of Christianity were of the lower and middle classes, always more sober in their apparel than the aristocracy.

THE husbandman that laboureth must be first partaker of the fruits.   (2 Tim. 2 : 6)

Agriculture was the basic occupation of man in antiquity, even more than in modern times; for, without scientific methods of production and in the absence of any source of power beyond that supplied by man and beast, the amount of food produced was usually barely sufficient to keep the population alive. Another factor which made cultivation of the soil imperative in every suitable spot was the difficulty experienced in transporting large quantities of produce from one country to another; the wheat trade of Egypt with Italy was an exception (see V.13: 105, 110). The feeding of the large cities, and above all of the capital, Rome, with its huge and unproductive population, presented an especially serious problem. For, since the Punic wars with their attendant ruin of the independent peasantry, the great Roman nobles had bought up the small cultivators and created huge estates *(latifundia)* which served mainly for the luxuries and pleasures of their owners. In his simile here, the apostle stresses the importance of the farmers and their right to their produce, a right endangered by the taxes and dues exacted by the landlord. The illustration shows a farmer of Italy, Titus Paconius Caledus, the son of Titus, supervising the bringing in of the harvest. He is standing on the right with a book of accounts in his hand, watching his servants bring in the produce of his farm.

BUT in a great house there are not only vessels of gold and of silver, but also of wood and of earth . . .   (2 Tim. 2 : 20)

In listing the materials of which the vessels found in the great houses of antiquity were made, the apostle states facts amply confirmed by modern archaeological discoveries. The finest vessels were of gold and silver; not many of these have survived, because the precious metals were naturally the first objects to be stolen and melted down. But, even so, there has been a series of finds of treasures of gold and silver ware. The illustration shows a vase from the famous find made at Hildesheim in Northern Germany. It consisted of the complete table service of a Roman noble — 74 pieces in all. The treasure was probably booty taken by the Germans from the Romans in the first century A.D. and buried in the earth. The costliness and variety of the objects (one of which, a mixing krater, ornamented in relief with plants and animals, is reproduced on the right) vividly illustrates the verse above. Pottery vessels were, of course, much more common; they formed the staple household ware and their sherds are found in great quantities on every ancient site. The example shown right, is a spindle-shaped bottle, typical of the Herodian period, the time of Jesus and St. Paul. Wooden vessels have only rarely been preserved in the Holy Land; they are much more numerous in Egypt with its drier climate. The example shown here on the left is a small wooden box, found in one of the caves near the Dead Sea which served in the second cent. A.D. as places of refuge for Jews hiding from the Romans.

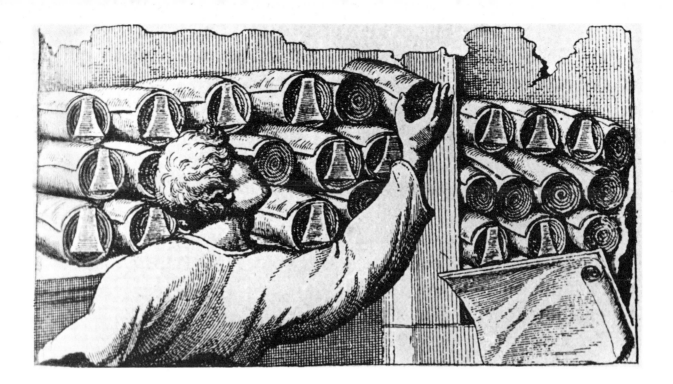

THE cloke that I left at Troas with Carpus, when thou comest, bring with thee, and the books, but especially the parchments. (2 Tim. 4 : 13)

Even if St. Paul could be demonstrated not to be the author of 1 and 2 Timothy as they have come down to us the passage 2 Tim. 4 : 9-21 is regarded as a genuine Pauline fragment. The cloak left by him at Troas is called *phelone*, a rare word which is generally assumed to be a corruption of *phainole*, corresponding to the Latin *paenula*. This was a mantle made of coarse wool, usually with a hood attached, which was the normal dress of the common people in the Roman empire, and especially of travellers (see the illustration below taken from a Pompeian design, showing a traveller settling his accounts with an inn-keeper). An apostle, whose life was spent in journeying from one place to another, was especially in need of such a warm and comfortable garment to protect him from the vicissitudes of the road. Of still greater importance to St. Paul, however, were the books, and especially the parchments, that he had left behind. The books *(biblia)* were rolls of papyrus, the usual material for ancient books; they were kept rolled together, each with an identifying tag, as we can see in the illustration above, which is a reproduction of a relief showing a librarian looking for a roll. The parchments (in Greek *membrana*) were thin skins of animals (mostly sheep or goats) prepared for writing. As they were more durable than papyrus, they were used for more important writings, and were usually bound together in the form of a book (not a roll), the so-called *codex*. The parchments which St. Paul was so anxious to receive were perhaps sacred texts, most useful in missionary work.

E XHORT servants to be obedient unto
their own masters . . .   (Titus 2 : 9)

As we have already seen, the social message of early Christianity was not revolutionary; it stressed the relative unimportance of social divisions between Greeks and barbarians, slaves and free men (see p. 12), as compared to the importance of eternal salvation through faith. Kings and those in authority are to be prayed for (p. 49), although they are but lords and masters of this world. In the same way the institution of slavery is not condemned, but a mitigation of its initial harshness is sought. Slaves are to obey their master. This was not always an easy command to follow, and sometimes the slave took matters into his own hands and became a fugitive. Formerly the runaway slave, when caught, had been cruelly punished by being branded. In Christian times this brutal branding was replaced by a badge, like the one illustrated here on the left. It reads "I have escaped, hold me, if you return me to my master (follows a name) you shall receive a *solidus* (gold coin)". The badge is a round piece of metal, 2¾ in. in diameter, provided with a hole for a string by which it was attached to the neck of the runaway.

To speak evil of no man, to be no brawlers . . .   (Titus 3 : 2)

The lower classes of Roman society, with their lack of any intellectual interests, naturally tended to various types of gross enjoyment and pastimes requiring no mental effort. Such inclinations were easily satisfied by frequenting the numerous taverns with their facilities for drinking and gambling. The writer on many occasions warns the members of the communities he has founded to abstain from this type of life, with its attendant moral dangers. A vivid illustration of the brawling which was the almost inevitable accompaniment of visits to such low haunts is provided by the illustration on p. 54, left, and above, reproduced from a Pompeian painting. It shows two scenes of gambling and its consequences. In the first picture on the left the two gamblers begin to quarrel about the results of a throw; in the second they start fighting and insulting each other in the grossest terms, while the terrified landlord begs them to "Go, quarrel outside". The artist has not given us a third picture showing the end of the quarrel, but it can easily be imagined (see p. 24). The second scene is now defaced, but a design, made while it was entire, gives an idea of how it looked originally.

ND to our beloved Apphia, and
Archippus our fellow soldier, and to the
church in thy house.   (Philem. 2)

The emerging Christian communities, small in numbers, despised by the masses, occasionally persecuted by the Roman authorities, and in constant conflict with the local Jewish synagogue, were naturally not over-anxious to advertise their existence. Their places of worship were therefore mostly located in the interior of private houses which, if built in the prevailing Mediterranean style, with the rooms grouped round a courtyard and enclosed on all sides, could not easily be looked into by an unfriendly eye. There was such a church in the house of Philemon of Colossae, a man of standing and the owner of a slave Onesimus; the latter is here returned to his master with a message from St. Paul. We can form an idea of the external aspect of such a domestic church from another of the same kind uncovered in the excavations of Dura-Europus on the River Euphrates, and dating to the third cent. A.D. (see plan above). This church was indistinguishable from a private house; it was entered from the street by way of a colonnaded court and consisted of a chapel, with walls covered by wall-paintings (reproduced above), a big room for the love-meal (agape) of the community, and an assembly hall, made by joining together two separate rooms, with a seat for the head of the community, probably a bishop. In the first centuries of the Christian era most Christian worship, even in times of relative quiet, must have taken place in such domestic churches.

SAT down on the right
hand of the Majesty . . .
(Heb. 1 : 3)

In placing Jesus "on the right hand of majesty" the author of the Epistle to the Hebrews evidently had before his eyes the public appearance of the Roman emperor or a high magistrate. It was the general Roman usage for all officials of the republic, not excepting the emperor, to have assessors who sat with them during the judicial proceedings and advised them on the verdict to be pronounced, although legally only the magistrate himself was responsible for the decision, his advisers being there merely in a consultative capacity. Nevertheless, the advice of learned jurists given to an emperor unlearned in the law must have been fairly decisive; in the later empire the right to be consulted was granted to eminent lawyers even when not in attendance on the emperor. Reproduced here is a representation of the emperor in council from the Arch of Constantine ar Rome. (As we know, the head of the emperor was changed when the reliefs were taken down from their original setting and placed in their present position). The original reliefs seem to have depicted Marcus Aurelius seated on the magistrate's curule chair and surrounded by his assessors; he is shown distributing some sort of favours to the populace assembled at the foot of his tribunal.

THOU art a priest for ever after the order of Melchisedec.   (Heb. 5 : 6)

Melchisedec is mentioned in Genesis 14 : 18 as "king of Salem and priest of God most high" (See Vol. 1, p. 50).
He received Abraham with bread and wine after the victory over the allied kings, Chedorlaomer and others,
and received a tithe of the booty. The Canaanite king-priest, whose dynasty continued to reign in Jerusalem at
least till the time of the Israelite conquest (cf. Josh. 10 : 1, 26) was transformed later on into the prototype of
a priestly ruler of superior order; the kings of the Davidic dynasty were assured in Psalm 110 : 4: "The Lord
has sworn and will not repent: Thou art a priest for ever after the order of Melchisedec".
In the epistle to the Hebrews (chapters 5-7) the argument is taken further. In attempting to show that Jesus
had superseded the Jewish high priest, the author first argues that there was a priesthood in the order of Melchisedec parallel with, but superior to, that descended from Aaron. For as Abraham paid tithe to Melchisedec, he
admitted his superiority; and as Levi and his descendants the priests were as yet unborn, they were represented
by their ancestor Abraham in admitting this superiority. The name and title of Melchisedec, interpreted as "king
of righteousness" and "King of Salem, which is king of peace", were in the eyes of the author attributable to
Jesus.
The meeting of Abraham and Melchisedec is represented in a sixth-century illuminated manuscript of Genesis
(the so-called "Genesis of Vienna"). Abraham approaches on the left, his hands covered,to accept the wine and
bread; Melchisedec comes towards him from the right. He is dressed in the raiment of the Byzantine emperor,
with diadem, purple mantle and red shoes; he carries a loaf and a jug. Behind Melchisedec is a symbolic representation of the Temple.

A MINISTER of the sanctuary, and of the true tabernacle, which the LORD pitched, and not man.

(Heb. 8 : 2)

Following his general line of reasoning, the author of the Epistle to the Hebrews describes Jesus as the minister of the true tabernacle, set up by the Lord, as opposed to the Tabernacle which accompanied the Israelites on their wandering through the desert and was the work of man, although prepared by divine command (see Vol. 2, p. 44). The Tabernacle, which was later transferred to Shiloh and superseded by the Temple of Solomon, was throughout the ages revered by the Jews as the visible symbol of the pristine purity of their faith in the desert wanderings. One of the earliest representations of the Tabernacle in its wanderings is to be found on the frieze of the Capernaum synagogue (see V.13:20). probably from the late second cent. A.D. This object was for a long time misunderstood; some scholars considered it to represent a wagon, or the carriage which was a prerogative of the Jewish Patriarch in Roman times. However, since the discovery of the synagogue frescoes of Dura Europus it has become clear that the relief represents the Tabernacle during its wanderings in the desert. It has here, as at Dura, the shape of a temple mounted on wheels, and corresponds to the carriages shaped like sanctuaries in which the Romans transported the images of their gods from one place to another.

THEY were stoned, they were sawn asunder, were tempted, were slain with the sword . . .   (Heb. 11 : 37)

The author of the Epistle to the Hebrews seems to refer here to the legendary death of the Prophet Isaiah. According to this legend, which has been preserved both in Jewish midrashic literature and in a Greek apocryphal work called "The Ascension of Isaiah", the prophet was put to death on the orders of the idolatrous king Manasseh of Judah, the unworthy successor of the pious Hezekiah whom Isaiah served as counsellor. Isaiah is said to have been put between two halves of a tree trunk and sawn asunder. A Coptic painting (reproduced above) found in the necropolis of Bagawat, in the oasis of el-Khargeh (Egypt), shows the prophet in a sitting position with two executioners, one on either side, sawing at him. A Greek inscription "Isaiah" over his head identifies the subject. The painting dates to the fifth century A.D.

BEHOLD, we put bits in the horses' mouths, that they may obey us; and we turn about their whole body. Behold also the ships, which though they be so great, and are driven of fierce winds, yet are they turned about with a very small helm, whithersoever the governor listeth.

(Jas. 3 : 3-4)

In order to illustrate his thesis of the dangers inherent in the wrong use of such a small organ of the human body as the tongue, the author has recourse to two comparisons. The first is with the bit put in the horse's mouth, a small piece of metal which nevertheless governs the movement of the large animal. Bits have been found in excavations from the time of the Hyksos invasion of Palestine and Egypt; the invaders, whose strength lay in their chariots, had learnt to tame the horse and control it by the use of bits. The example reproduced below shows a bit found at Pompeii. Similar to the bit is the ship's helm (see illustration above). In antiquity ships were generally small (see V.13 : 105) and, instead of the elaborate rudder-mechanism used in modern vessels, they were steered by oars of larger than usual size; two such oars were passed through the stern, and the desired direction was given to the vessel by moving them to the right or left. Reproduced above is a ship on a Late Roman sarcophagus with the steering oars clearly visible.

YE have heard of the patience of Job . . .   (Jas. 5 : 11)

The book of Job, one of the most profound as well as one of the most poetical books of the Bible, must have recommended itself to the early Christians as an example of sufferings meekly and patiently borne. In their tribulations they found encouragement in the example of Job's patience and his ultimate reward by God, along with that of the husbandman who patiently awaits his crops; all the greater will be the reward at the coming of the Lord. This reference to Job in the Letter of St. James has undoubtedly led to the inclusion of Job among the representations of the just in the stock themes of early Christian art. The illustration shows the sufferer sitting on the ash-heap (Job 2 : 8) with his wife and a friend standing by to console him. The relief is part of the decoration of the sarcophagus of Junius Bassus, prefect of the city of Rome, who died on the 25th August 359. The coffin can thus be dated exactly. Its façade is divided into two storeys, with columns separating the various scenes, each of which is surmounted by a gable or an arch. The scenes shown include, besides Job, Adam and Eve, the Sacrifice of Isaac, Daniel in the lions' den, and several scenes from the lives of Jesus, St. Peter and St. Paul.

WHOSE adorning let it not be that outward adorning of plaiting the hair, and of wearing of gold, or of putting on of apparel.

(1 Pet. 3 : 3)

Female fashions in Roman society in the first century A.D. entered on a phase of fanciful adornment, in contrast with the simpler fashion of the preceding Augustan era and of the Antonine period which followed. Already in the time of Nero fashionable ladies began to pile up their hair in monstrously high curled coiffures; and in the succeeding Flavian period this fashion reached a pitch of absurdity equalled perhaps only in eighteenth century Europe. Reproduced on the right is a portrait bust, supposed to represent Julia the daughter of the emperor Titus. Her hair is dressed as a veritable tower of locks piled high up over her forehead; such a construction could hardly have been held in position without some inside support, probably furnished by false hair. In view of such a style of hairdressing we can understand how Roman ladies passed hours in the hands of the slaves who prepared their coiffures, a frivolous waste of time strongly condemned by the apostles. The wearing of costly jewelry and of gorgeous raiment, on the other hand, is not bound up with any special fashion; in the Orient it has existed since time immemorial, witness the strictures of the prophets, especially Isaiah (see Vol. 6, pp. 22-23) and Amos (see V.8:40). The lady Bithnaia represented in a fresco from Dura-Europus, with her high tiara, abundance of ornaments and purple garment, is but one example of the many that could be given in this connection.

WE have also a more sure word of prophecy; whereunto ye do well that ye take heed, as unto a light that shineth in a dark place, until the day dawn . . .   (2 Pet. 1 : 19)

As we have seen in another connection (cf. V.12:31 and 69), the only form of artificial light in ancient times was that provided either by wicks burning in oil, or by candles or torches; in any case the quantity of illumination, even when a large number of lamps were placed together, was very small. The same applies also to the streets; apart from nights on which the moon shone, there was no street-lighting at all. Anyone who ventured out into the night had to carry a lantern, and such a light was highly welcome in a dark place. The example reproduced here was found at Pompeii. The bronze body of the lantern is suspended by chains from a handle; inset into the bronze at the bottom there is a wick which is fed by oil supplied, drop by drop, from a receptacle. The frame of the lamp contained some transparent material which allowed the light of the wick to shine through. The lantern is marked with the name of the maker or owner.

FOR the time past of our life may suffice us to have wrought the will of the Gentiles, when we walked in lasciviousness, lusts, excess of wine, revellings, banquetings, and abominable idolatries.

(1 Pet. 4 : 3)

The pagan religions of antiquity regarded man and nature as fundamentally one; the gods, men, animals, trees, sea and earth were blended in a way which endowed anything in nature with divine approval. The Hellenes, who were the leading devotees of this pantheistic creed, were thus able to rise to the highest peaks of a lofty idealism, but at the same time, especially when influenced by the ancient Oriental mystery religions, they could sink into natural brutishness. Certain religious festivals in particular, combined with banquets, could end in orgies which released man's worst instincts. In marked constrast to this pantheism, both Judaism and Chrisianity adopted a dualistic attitude, sharply distinguishing God from the world or devil, and regarded all forms of sensual indulgence as abominable idolatries to be shunned by all true believers. Two examples of such orgiastic worship are given here: one — on the right — is the sacrifice to the Egyptian goddess Isis as depicted in a Pompeian painting. This Egyptian goddess was enormously popular with the Romans of the first century A.D., and was worshipped in particular by the women. We see, in the middle, an altar with horns, on which incense is smoking; worshippers approach the steps of the temple, while priests with shaven heads play the sistrum and pray on their knees. The second example (on the left) is from the design on an Attic vase of the second half of the fifth century B.C., showing the orgiastic dance of nymphs in honour of the god Dionysus.

LITTLE children, keep yourselves from idols . . .   (1 John 5 : 21)

St. John concludes his First Epistle, in which he has discussed the relations of God to light, justice and love successively, with a final warning against idolatry, addressing the faithful as "little children". The dangers of idol-worship were naturally greater with children used to following the teaching of their fathers than with adults who could reason for themselves. Quite possibly St. John had in mind the common artistic representations of children worshipping Greek gods, like the one in the procession reproduced above from a fresco found at Rome. One of the favourite subjects of ancient art was the portrayal of children (usually indentified with Cupid or Amor, the child-god of love and son of Venus) practising the various professions or in general behaving like grown-ups; the contrast between the childish figures and the seriousness of their acts was found especially attractive. The painting here in which children are seen worshipping Diana and forming a procession, might well have been executed in the same spirit.

TREES whose fruit withereth, without fruit, twice dead, plucked up by the roots.

(Jude 12)

In its polemics against the teachings and practice of those who had perverted the doctirne of God's forgiveness of sins into an excuse for immoral living, the pseudonymous letter of St. Jude cites Cain (godlessness), Balaam (cupidity) and Korah (disobedience) as prototypes from whose punishment Christians may deduce the certainty of the awesome judgment these present sinners are bringing down upon their heads. They are likened to clouds without water, carried about by winds; trees whose fruit withereth, twice dead; waves of the ocean, full of sound, casting up the foam of shame; wandering stars, fated to burn out into nothingness. A barren tree as a figure of wretchedness was used in Isa. 56 : 3, Jer. 8 : 13, Matt. 3 : 10. In the dry districts of Judaea, especially, a barren tree was a common sight (see illustration above).

REVELATION

I AM Alpha and Omega . . .   (Rev. 1 : 8)

The last book of the New Testament is the Revelation of St. John the Divine; its subject is the Second coming of Christ, the Day of Judgment and the End of the World, to be followed by the New Heaven and New Earth; but before this consummation the wicked are to perish and humanity — save the elect — be decimated by the messengers of divine wrath. The book of Revelation contains a number of symbolical allusions to contemporary politics, the reality of Roman power, the wicked emperor and his predecessors, the danger of invasion from the East, and similar subjects. In the first chapter of the Book, God is symbolically described as the Alpha and Omega, the first and last letters of the Greek alphabet, and hence by implication the first and last of things, as all the secrets of the universe can be expressed by these letters and what comes between them. On account of this verse, the letters Alpha and Omega are usually added to the cross in many works of early Christian art. The example chosen above is taken from the sixth century mosaic in the church of Saint Apollinare in Classe in Ravenna. Drawn on a background of stars in heaven is a golden cross studded with jewels, with the head of Christ in its centre. The letters Alpha and Omega appear to the left and right respectively of the horizontal arms of the cross.

AND being turned, I saw seven golden candlesticks.

(Rev. 1 : 12)

The Revelation begins with a vision connected with the seven principal churches of Asia, symbolized here by seven golden candlesticks. In the period following the destruction of Jerusalem in A.D. 70 the golden candlestick of the Temple (see Vol. 2, p. 47) became the recognized symbol of Judaism; here, however, it is still treated as the heavenly symbol of divine light (cf. Zechariah 4). Ancient representations of the candlestick, beginning with that on the Arch of Titus, are very numerous and the type seems to change with the ages. It appears sculptured in relief in Galilean synagogues (but without the predominant position it achieves later on), on Jewish lamps both from Palestine and the Diaspora, on gold glasses (see the illustration above of a gold glass found at Rome), on bone and ivory carvings and on the mosaic pavements of later synagogues, on Jewish coffins, and painted on the walls of Jewish catacombs. On the gold glass above the seven branched candlesticks are accompanied by the full array of Jewish ritual objects: the Ark of the Torah flanked by two lions, and below them the candlesticks accompanied by ram's horns *(shofar)*, citrons *(ethrog)*, a palm branch *(lulab)* and an oil jar.

THE seven stars are the angels of the seven churches: and the seven candlesticks which thou sawest, are the seven churches.

(Rev. 1 : 20)

The seven churches symbolized by the seven stars, seven angels and seven candlesticks, are listed in detail in the rest of the chapter. They are (see map) those of Ephesus, Smyrna, Pergamos, Thyatira, Sardis, Philadelphia and Laodicea. Some of these cities had been connected with the missionary activity of St. Paul. He himself had been active for a long time in Ephesus, the capital of Asia (see V.13:91); his disciple Epaphras had laboured in Laodicea (Col. 4 : 12, 13); and his convert Lydia was a native of Thyatira (Acts 16 : 14). The other churches, mentioned here for the first time, are those of Pergamos (see p. 75), the great trading city of Smyrna, Sardis, the ancient capital of the Lydian kingdom, and Philadelphia, one of the main road-junctions in the Hermus valley. All these were among the most important cities of the Roman province of Asia and, as we learn from this chapter, had Christian communities established in them at an early date; we may also presume that there were Jewish communities in all of them (see also next page).

Roman Roads _____

AND unto the angel of the church in Smyrna write . . .　　　　　　(Rev. 2 : 8)

The Smyrna which is mentioned as the second of the seven churches of Asia was the city refounded (near the ruins of an earlier Ionian colony) in the fourth cent. B.C. Its geographical position at the head of a deep bay ensured its commercial prosperity; loyal to Rome, it flourished under imperial rule and vied with Ephesus and Pergamon for the primacy of the province. It was allowed first to erect a Temple to Tiberius, Livia and the Senate and thus obtained the title of "Warden of the Temple". The Jewish community in Smyrna seems to have existed since Hellenistic times; numerous inscriptions attest its importance and wealth into the third century. It seems to have given special trouble to the Christians living in the town, and was singled out for blame at the end of the message here. The photograph shows the present harbour and city of Smyrna, looking north.

AND to the angel of the church in Pergamos write ... I know thy works, and where thou dwellest, even where Satan's seat is ...

(Rev. 2 : 12-13)

Pergamon ("Pergamos" here) rose to greatness as the capital of the royal dynasty of the Attalids (283-133 B.C.) who founded a powerful kingdom in the north-western corner of Asia Minor. The last ruler of the dynasty, Attalus III, bequeathed his kingdom to the Romans, and under them it became the nucleus of the province of Asia; Pergamon remained the capital of the province till the end of the first century B.C., when it was transferred to Ephesus. The Attalids had embellished their capital with splendid palaces, temples and other public buildings. The most famous of their works was the Great Altar of Zeus and Athene, erected by king Eumenes II (197-159 B.C.) in commemoration of Attalid victories over the Gauls. This building (see reconstruction above) stood on a large terrace overlooking the agora of the city. It measured 120 by 112 feet and consisted of a colonnaded court surrounded by walls on three sides, with an altar in its centre (see the reconstruction). Around the outer wall of the court ran the great frieze, 400 feet long and 7 ft. high, depicting the battle of the gods against the giants who attempted to storm Olympus. (The lower illustration shows the three-headed Hekate fighting a serpent-legged giant with a torch). The frieze is one of the most magnificent works of Hellenistic sculpture, and the deep impression it made on even a hostile beholder is still evident from the appellation "Satan's seat" given it here.

AND will give him a white stone . . . (Rev. 2 : 17)

The mystic "white stone" enumerated among the other objects passed on to the church of Pergamon is a sign of acquittal. A stone (*psephos* in Greek, also used for mosaic stones) was used for voting by the judges of the Athenian courts (occasionally beans were used instead of stones). To vote with a white stone meant acquittal, while a black stone stood for condemnation. The legendary origin of this custom goes back to the trial of Orestes, the son of Agamemnon king of Mycenae, in the Areopagos (seeV.13:87),the ancient supreme court of Athens. Orestes had avenged his father by killing Clytemnestra, his mother, and her paramour, Aegistheus. Pursued because of his matricide by the Erinnyes, the goddesses of vengeance, he stood his trial before the Athenian judges. As the votes were evenly divided, Pallas-Athene, who favoured him, threw in a white stone (the *calculus Minervae*) and thus got him acquitted. The illustration above (taken from a Greek vase of the painter Duris, c. 490 B.C.) shows the Greek heroes voting as to who should receive the arms of the dead Achilles ; Athena, standing behind the altar on which the stones are placed, decides in favour of Odysseus.

HE that overcometh,
the same shall be clothed
in white raiment ...
(Rev. 3 : 5)

White raiment was the hallowed garb of purity among the pagans, as well as among the Christians and Jews. Thus, the Israelite priests were dressed in white linen (Ex. 28 : 40-42); and white is the colour symbolic of purification from sins in Isa. 1 : 18. In the Gospels an angel who came to sit by Jesus' tomb (Mark 16 : 5) is dressed in a long white garment; and elsewhere in Revelation the armies of heaven appear in spotless white linen, riding on white horses (Rev. 19 : 11, 14). Representations of saints and martyrs in white raiment abound in early Christian art. The illustration chosen is earlier than most of these: it depicts the priests at Dura Europus (third cent. A.D.). On this fresco the chief priest and his assistant are both dressed in long white robes and are wearing a high conical cap of the same colour. In the religious philosophy of Philo personages enveloped in white light appear endowed with mystic-symbolic significance.

HIM that overcometh will I make a pillar in the temple of my God, and he shall go no more out: and I will write upon him the name of my God, and the name of the city of my God, which is New Jerusalem . . . (Rev. 3 : 12)

In the vision here recorded reference is made to writing upon the pillars of a temple. This custom is borne out by archaeological evidence from many ancient sites. Sometimes statues of prominent persons were placed against the upper part of a column and their names and titles written on the column underneath. At Palmyra, a whole street had been thus decorated; the statues have perished, but the inscriptions have remained. In other places, the name of the person dedicating the column was written on it. This was especially the custom in the Galilean synagogues of the third-fourth centuries A.D. Since the Jewish communities in Galilee had no members rich enough to donate a whole building, every benefactor gave part of the edifice, and his name was written on the part donated by him (see the inscription in memory of a donator on the "cathedra of Moses", V. 12:63). The illustration chosen here shows a column in the synagogue at Capernaum (see V. 13:20); it bears a dedication in Greek by Herod, the son of Mokimos, and his descendants. A second column is dedicated in Aramaic. Both prove that the custom of writing on pillars was a wide-spread one.

AND anoint thine eyes with eyesalve, that thou mayest see.
(Rev. 3 : 18)

Medicine in the Roman empire was not a regulated profession; anyone could practise it, and the better physicians succeeded mainly because of the higher class of client they were able to treat. Usually the physicians prepared their medicines themselves, but for certain special diseases they were provided by pharmacists who had compounded the specific or who had inherited the prescription. Such remedies were peddled throughout the length and breadth of the empire by itinerant vendors and marked with specially prepared stamps. Such stamps have been found in large quantities. They usually bear the name of the manufacturer or inventor, and the name of the malady against which the ointment was supposed to be effective. Oculists' salves occupy a prominent place among them. Reproduced here is one such stamp which marked, amongst other remedies, an eyesalve — obviously of the kind referred to above. Occasionally such remedies actually helped: Galen mentions among his prescriptions one entitled "Eyesalve applied by Florus to Antonia the mother of Drusus, when she was in danger of losing her eyesight through applications of other physicians".

Aᴺᴰ I saw in the right hand of him that sat on the throne a book written within and on the backside, sealed with seven seals.   (Rev. 5 : 1)

The sealing of written documents was intended to protect their contents from unauthorized eyes and, at the same time, to authenticate them. Prominent personages, such as emperors, had their own seals executed by engravers skilled enough to make the counterfeiting of the seal most difficult. We know, for example, that the emperor Augustus used to seal his letters with the image of Alexander the Great, specially cut for him by the famous engraver Dioscorides. Multiple sealings were used to safeguard signatures. As an example, one may mention the receipt books of the Pompeian banker, Lucius Caecilius Jucundus (see illustration below). These books consist of six pages, the outer ones (1 and 6) being blank, while 2 and 3 contain the text of the receipt which is sealed on page 4 by a series of seals, with the name of the witness recorded beside each. The figure of the book with the seven seals, which were broken one by one, must have been modelled on some such document, the implication being that the divine judgment against the world written on its pages was to remain a secret, till the time came to break the seals open.

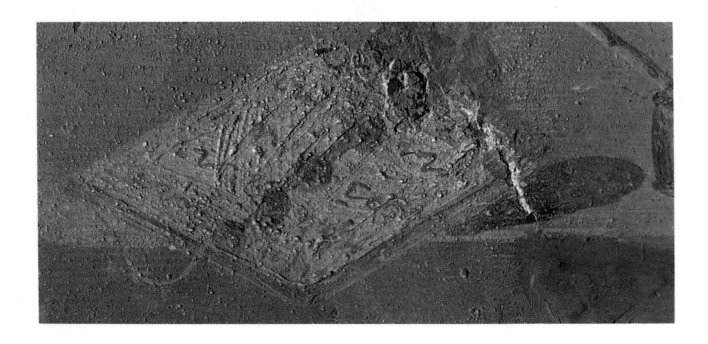

AND I saw, and behold a white horse: and he that sat on him had a bow; and a crown was given unto him: and he went forth conquering, and to conquer.　　　(Rev. 6 : 2)

The world in which the Book of Revelation was written was that of the Roman empire at the peak of its tremendous and apparently unshakeable power under the early emperors. The vision therefore dwells on the destruction of the nerve-centres of the existing order by the various enemies whom divine omnipotence could raise up against Rome. The first of these are the Parthians, those inveterate enemies first of the Hellenistic kingdoms, and then of the Romans who succeeded Hellenism and managed to save it at least as far as the River Euphrates. The Parthians were the successors of the ancient Persians in their struggles with the Seleucids, whom they gradually drove back from the highlands of Iran and, late in the second century, from Babylonia. In 54 B.C. they defeated a Roman army under the triumvir Crassus at Carrhae in Upper Mesopotamia, and thus saved themselves from Roman domination. Wars between the Romans and the Parthians continued throughout the centuries, with now one power gaining the upper hand, now the other. The peoples subject to Rome and restive under its yoke hoped for the Parthians to put an end to Roman rule. Thus, one of the Jewish sages who was opposed to Rome expressed the opinion that the days of the Messiah would come, if a Persian (Parthian) horse was seen tethered to the monuments of the Holy Land. The paintings at Dura Europus contain many representations of mounted Parthian horsemen (see above); their kings are usually portrayed as conquerors holding a bow, which was the Parthian weapon par excellence. The Parthians excelled especially in shooting from horseback, and could even shoot backwards when galloping in full retreat.

T·FLAVIS·BASSVS·MVCA
F·DANSALAE·EQ·ALAE·NOR
CORV·TVR·FABI·PVDENTIS
AN·XXXXVI·STP·XXVI·H·F·C

And there went out another horse that was red: and power was given to him that sat thereon to take peace from the earth, and that they should kill one another: and there was given unto him a great sword.

(Rev. 6 : 4)

The second rider on a red horse seems to symbolize civil war. If the assumption is correct that the Revelation was written in the time of the emperor Domitian, the author would vividly remember the convulsion which shook the Roman empire when the emperor Nero (see p. 49), by his madness, finally provoked a general uprising against his rule. Within the short span of one year no fewer than four emperors were proclaimed and three of them, Galba, Otho and Vitellius, perished by assassination, suicide or execution. The various provincial armies vied with each other in raising their commanders to the status of emperor, in the hope that their candidate would prevail and that they would enjoy his largesse. In the end Vespasian, the contender chosen by the armies of the East, was victorious and established the Flavian dynasty; but in the civil war of the years 68/69 the instability of the imperial government had been fully exposed and all the enemies of Rome could hope for a repetition of similar events. The rider of the red horse was to cause the Romans "to kill one another"; his great sword was a typical Roman cavalry weapon, the *spatha* (as distinguished from the short Spanish sword of the Roman infantry). Reproduced in the illustration is the tombstone of Titus Flavius Bassus, son of Dansala, a cavalryman of the Norican troop, who died at the age of 46 after 26 years of service. He is seen mounted on his horse and trampling down a fallen enemy. His spear is in his right hand and his long sword hangs at his side.

A ND I beheld, and lo, a black horse; and he that sat on him had a pair of balances in his hand. And I heard a voice in the midst of the four beasts say, A measure of wheat for a penny, and three measures of barley for a penny; and see thou hurt not the oil and the wine.

(Rev. 6 : 5-6)

The third rider, on a black horse, stands for a natural disaster — that of famine (cf. Acts 11 : 28) — which is to overwhelm existing society. In the primitive conditions of production, and especially transport, prevailing in antiquity, a drought and failure of crops in one place could only with difficulty be remedied by shipping the produce of another place to the areas affected. The rider is enjoined not to touch the wine and oil, as these are not essential to human life. He is given a balance (called in Greek "a pair", from the pair of scales which, together with the bar and tongue, constituted the normal balance — see the illustration above, one of the balances found at Pompeii). The balance was used for weighing; here, however, it is largely symbolical, because dearth is expressed not in terms of weight, but of measure. The Greeks and Romans employed standard measures, inscribed with the quantity they contained. The example reproduced here was found at Carvoran (England) and belongs to the reign of Domitian, the time when the Revelation was written. It is marked with the date and a line showing a capacity of 16 sextarii — equalling one modius, or "measure". The measure mentioned here is the *choinix,* calculated at 1.08 litres or .98 quarts. One choinix of wheat was sufficient for one day; but as the pay for a day's work was only one denarius (see Matt. 20 : 9) — here translated "penny" — it was outrageous to have to pay a whole day's wage for one measure only. Barley, of course, which was consumed only in time of need and was — except in poor districts — normally reserved for horses or donkeys, was three times as cheap as wheat even in times of famine.

CLOTHED with white robes, and palms in their hands. (Rev. 7 : 9)

The vision of the blessed stresses the purity of the elect, symbolized by their white robes (see p. 77) and their ultimate victory, symbolized by the palm branches (see also V.13:56). Palm branches were, from early times, presented to the victors in Greek athletic contests, together with the crown (see p. 29). They served as a symbol of triumph on the occasion of the Maccabaean conquests, as well as at the triumphal entry of Jesus into Jerusalem. There are many illustrations showing victorious athletes holding palm branches, or judges in a contest standing by with a palm branch to be handed to the victor. In the statue reproduced here a charioteer, the winner of a circus race, is seen holding a palm branch. In the symbolical significance given to the term *agon* (contest) by St. Paul, the struggle of the believer with the world around him was likened to the contest in the palaestra. The victor, i.e. the steadfast martyr, who sealed his faith with his life, received a crown and a palm branch in the other world. Such scenes are frequently represented on catacomb paintings and in church mosaics.

 AND another angel came and stood at the altar, having a golden censer... (Rev. 8 : 3)

The burning of incense, i.e. spices which gave off a cloud of fragrant smoke, before the altars of the gods was common to most nations of antiquity. The importance attached to this rite can be gauged from the fact that the raw materials required were quite often imported from remote lands (in particular Southern Arabia), regardless of cost. The Books of Exodus and Leviticus contain long and detailed descriptions of the elements from which incense was to be compounded (see Vol. 2, p. 60). The incense placed on the altar — see the reproduction above, from a third century painting found at Dura Europus, representing a sacrifice made by a Roman tribune and his soldiers — was burnt in special containers called censers. These were of two kinds: the closed type which was swung at the end of a chain and has been adopted by the Church; and the open type, apparently the more ancient, which is illustrated here. It consisted of a flat shovel on which glowing coals were heaped (see below). To prevent the heat of the metal burning the hand of the sacrificer, the handle was coated with some heat-resistant material. The incense itself was either held in the hand (see Vol. 1, p. 19), or kept piled up in two flat receptacles attached to the two upper corners of the incense-shovel from where it was taken between pinched fingers and thrown upon the coals. Representations of such shovels are common in mosaic synagogue pavements, accompanying the seven-branched candlestick.

ND there was given me a reed like unto a rod: and the angel stood, saying, Rise and measure the temple of God, and the altar, and them that worship therein.   (Rev. 11 : 1)

In several prophetic visions in the Old Testament an angel or messenger of God appears with a measuring rod, to mark out the ground-plan of the future Temple (Ezek. 40 : 3; Zech. 2 : 1). The instruments referred to in these books were, in all probability, similar to those which we find represented on Egyptian or Babylonian monuments. However, the measuring rod seen by the author of Revelation in his vision was more probably of the type employed by the Romans, which is illustrated on the right. This rod is made of metal, with a hinge in the middle; its full length is one Roman foot. Of the four faces of the rod, the broad outer one is divided into 16 digits; the large inner face has 8 palms marked on it, four on each side of the hinge; and one of the two narrower faces is divided into 12 unciae. In this way the Roman measuring rod enabled its user to subdivide the foot by 8, 12 and 16, as required. Other similar instruments, made of bone and marked with dots, have also been found.

AND their dead bodies shall lie in the street of the great city . . .   (Rev. 11 : 8)

The dead bodies lying in the "streets" of the great city obviously refer to a disaster which is to overtake the city of Rome. Instead of the usual word for street, the Greek original here reads *plateia,* meaning "broad street". At the time when Revelation was written, the imperial city had begun to be transformed by the building activities of successive emperors. In particular, the area north of the old Roman Forum had been developed by a series of new fora, beginning with that of Julius Caesar in which stood the temple of Venus Genetrix, the legendary ancestress of the Julian family. Then Augustus built another forum with the Temple of Mars the Avenger (of the assassination of Julius Caesar); Vespasian built a third with the temple of Peace; and Nerva added a fourth, small forum. But all these were surpassed by the forum of Trajan, with its large semi-circular wings (see illustration above). The building and town-planning activities which changed the face of imperial Rome justified the title of "the Great City" given it in this verse.

AND I stood upon the sand of the sea, and saw a beast rise up out of the sea, having seven heads and ten horns, and upon his horns ten crowns . . .

(Rev. 13 : 1)

The vision of the beast with many heads and horns, as described here, is clearly related to the similar vision of Daniel (Chap. 7); only here we have to understand the reference to the Roman empire and its vassal states, instead of to the Hellenistic kingdoms. The seven heads are apparently the seven emperors who appear also in chap. 17 (see pp. 94-95): the ten heads wearing ten crowns are most probably the vassal kings of Rome. In general, the Romans tried as far as possible to avoid direct rule, especially in the case of the East with its long-established political institutions. A few dynasties which were too big and powerful to acquiesce in Roman overlordship (such as those of the Antigonids in Macedonia, the Seleucids in Syria and the Ptolemies in Egypt) were deposed; but minor rulers, if sufficiently pliant and in control of peoples inclined to revolt, were left in the possession of their thrones. Only gradually, in the course of the first century A.D., were these vassal kingdoms absorbed one by one. In the time of Augustus, a fringe of such vassal states protected the eastern borders of the Empire. They included the Bosphoran kingdom in the Crimea, Colchis in the Caucasus, the kingdoms of Armenia, Pontus, Cappadocia and Commagene in Asia Minor, Judaea under Herod, Chalcis and the Nabataean kingdom in Syria and Arabia, and Mauretania in Africa. One of the kings of Commagene, Antiochus I (69-34 B.C.), erected a magnificent monument in Nimrud Dagh, with statues and reliefs representing himself and his ancestors. One of these reliefs (reproduced above) portrays this Antiochus, with the god Mithras.

To receive a mark in their right hand, or in their foreheads. (Rev. 13 : 16)

The seal (Greek *charagma*) is applied to the elect to mark them on their right hand or forhead. The writer alludes to the well known custom of applying such seals — with the name and year of the reigning emperor — to letters of purchase and similar documents. One such seal, dated to the thirty-fifth year of Augustus (A.D. 5-6) and inscribed "In the year 35 of Caesar. The Secretariat", is reproduced here. It is made from soft limestone and is in mirror-writing, so as to reproduce the wording on the documents stamped in the right way. The dating made it necessary to prepare a new seal every year; hence the soft and provisional character of the stone which was used for this kind of seal.

THRUST in thy sharp sickle, and gather the clusters of the vine of the earth; for her grapes are fully ripe.   (Rev. 14 : 18)

The necessity of cutting the grape-clusters from the vine neatly and quickly, without injuring the delicate fruit led to the introduction of a specially sharp curved sickle for the use of vintagers (see illustration, above right) We see this sickle in use in a vintage scene reproduced on a sixth century mosaic pavement, found in the ruins of the monastery of Lady Mary at Beth-Shean. Depicted in the mosaic, within a framework of winding trellises which form circular medallions, are villagers cutting the grapes and carrying them to the wine-press in baskets. The man in the middle right medallion is holding a sharp sickle in his right hand and a big bunch of grapes in his left. The proportions are not exact, as in most Byzantine pavements; the artist was more interested in making his meaning clear than in giving each object its proper relative size. It is to such an operation that St. John compares the gathering of the vine of the earth — "for her grapes are fully ripe".

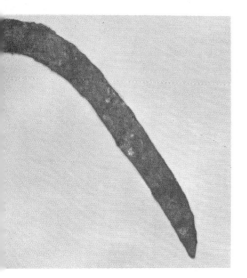

ND the sixth angel poured out his vial upon the great river Euphrates; and the water thereof was dried up, that the way of the kings of the east might be prepared.

(Rev. 16 : 12)

As in a previous verse, the author of Revelation here voices the aspirations of the oppressed Orientals and their desire to see the hated Roman power humbled before the Parthian kings of the East (see also p. 81). The River Euphrates, which formed the boundary between the two empires (for a view of the river see Vol. 2, p. 110) will suddenly dry up, thus in an instant removing the security of the Roman frontier behind it and giving the Parthians an unobstructed passage into the Roman province of Syria and beyond. This vision took some time to realize; it was only in the third century A.D. that the re-invigorated Persian empire, under its new Sassanian dynasty, came to serious grips with the Romans. The greatest moment in Sassanian history was the surrender of the emperor Valerian in A.D. 260 to the Persian king Sapor I, after a defeat in battle. Even before that the Persians had successfully invaded Syria and taken its capital Antioch in 255. This moment of triumph is represented on a rock relief at Naqsh-i Rustam showing Sapor I on his horse, with the Roman emperor kneeling at his feet.

AND he gathered them together into a place called in the Hebrew tongue Armageddon.
(Rev. 16 : 16)

The place of the last battle of the kings of this earth is described as Armageddon, which is a corruption of Har Mageddon or the "Mountain of Megiddo". This site, now identified with Tell el-Mutesellim at the point where the Valley of 'Iron and the Via Maris (Sea Road) debouch into the Valley of Esdraelon, was not inhabited at the time when the Revelation was written. Its strategic position, however, was still important; the Roman camp of the Sixth Legion was placed by Hadrian at near-by Legio (Lajjun), later on the city of Maximianupolis (see Vol. 8, p. 96). The broad expanse of the Valley of Esdraelon at the foot of the mountain (see view above), and the vital importance of the great trade-routes crossing it, seem to have influenced the choice of this place as the locality of the last battle. Possibly also memories of the great conflict between Josiah king of Judah and Pharaoh Necho may have contributed to this localization; for it is hardly likely that the still older battle at Megiddo in the time of Thotmes III of Egypt could have still been remembered in the first century A.D.

ND I saw a woman sit upon a scarlet coloured beast, full of names of blasphemy, having seven heads and ten horns. And the woman was arrayed in purple and scarlet colour, and decked with gold and precious stones and pearls . . .   (Rev. 17 : 3-4)

After the opening of the book with the seven seals, followed by the revelation of the great wonders of heaven and the coming of the seven angels with the seven last plagues, there appears the great enemy of god, Rome — thinly disguised under the appellation of "Babylon the Great". The imperial city is represented as a woman arrayed in purple and scarlet, and riding upon a scarlet beast. The components of this vision are obviously taken from the female statues personifying the great cities, or rather their tutelary goddesses or Tyches. From the time that the sculptor Eutychides created the prototype of such a goddess in his famous work representing the Tyche of Antioch, the personification of cities as dignified females wearing mural crowns became a generally accepted convention. There were local variations: thus Alexandria, the great port of Egypt, is represented wearing a crown formed by ships; and Rome, the warrior city, appears with helmet and breastplate, like a second Minerva (see also the next page). The illustration below, which is a reproduction of a painting found on the premises of one Verecundus, a cloth-maker in the "Street of Abundance" at Pompeii, shows another such symbolical image. It is the Venus of Pompeii, majestically draped in blue and crowned with gold, riding on a chariot drawn by elephants, with Cupid in attendance on her and winged genii hovering to their right and left. This hieratic figure, which recalls those of the Oriental gods, is of a type not unlike the vision of "Babylon the Great" in the Revelation.

THE seven heads are seven mountains, on which the woman sitteth. And there are seven kings: five are fallen, and one is, and the other is not yet come; and when he cometh, he must continue a short space. And the beast that was, and is not, even he is the eighth . . .

(Rev. 17 : 9-11)

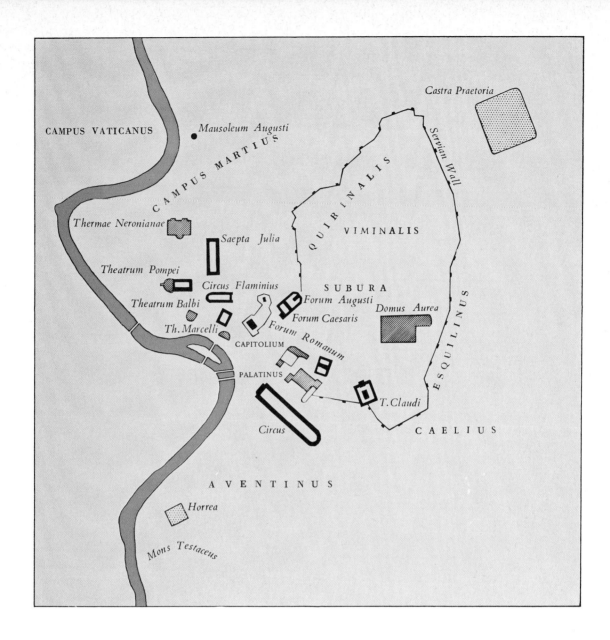

The city of Rome was founded beside the ford of the River Tiber nearest to the sea. The first settlement was built on a hill called the Palatine (see map on p. 95). Then the steep hill of the Capitol was crowned with a castle. In the time of the Republic five other hills (Aventine, Caelius, Esquiline, Viminal and Quirinal) were included within the city walls; they were all situated in the plain adjoining the ford across the Tiber (where later on the oldest bridge over the river was erected). Although imperial Rome extended far beyond these original seven hills, including parts of those on the left bank of the Tiber and various others still more distant, it retained its traditional designation as the "City of the Seven Hills"; and the same number of hills was later on assigned to its successor, Constantinople.

The interpretation of the mystic number of the seven kings (emperors) of Rome referred to here depends on the date assigned to the composition of the Book of Revelation. If we assume that the "beast that was and is not" is Domitian, then the five fallen kings would be the five emperors of the Julio-Claudian dynasty (see their coins above): Augustus (31 B.C. - 14 A.D. — upper left); Tiberius (14-37 — upper centre); Caligula (37-41 — upper right); Claudius (41-54 — lower left) and Nero (54-68 — lower centre). The "one that is" would be Vespasian (69-79 — lower right) — (omitting the three short-lived emperors of the civil war year 68-69, viz.: Galba, Otho and Vitellius). The one who "is to come and rule for a short time" would be Titus (79-81), to be followed by the "beast", Domitian (81-96).

ᴀɴᴅ the woman which thou sawest is that great city,
which reigneth over the kings of the earth.

(Rev. 17 : 18)

The goddess Roma, the incarnation of the city which became an empire, is here revealed as the true identity
of the "Babylon" in the text. As long as Rome was a republic, the guardian spirit of the state appeared on its
coins in the shape of a woman adorned with jewels and wearing a winged helmet surmounted by a griffin.
This symbol was transformed in the Orient into a goddess and worshipped together with the emperor. The representations of this patron deity were of two types: one that of the warrior goddess, modelled on Minerva or
Pallas Athene, or sometimes even appearing as an Amazon with helmet, high boots, spear and shield; and the
other, that of a city Tyche, with a mural crown (see p. 95). The illustration above, which is a reproduction of
the interior of a gilt silver bowl, found with the Hildesheim treasure (see p. 52), shows a compromise between
the two. Roma is here represented in the dress of a matron, with *stola* (robe) and *palla* (mantle), but wearing
the helmet of Minerva surmounted by a griffon flanked by two sphinxes, and leaning on a shield.

ND every shipmaster, and all the company in ships, and sailors, and as many as trade by sea, stood afar off.

(Rev. 18 : 17)

One of the results of the fall of Babylon-Rome will be the cessation of its maritime trade. To understand why this is singled out as the sure sign of disaster one has to appreciate the basic facts of the imperial city's existence. Its population was swollen by an enormous number of aliens, many of them slaves or freedmen, all of whom relied for their maintenance on the imperial bounty. Any failure of this bounty was, therefore, fraught with danger for the emperor and his court. Only by supplies of wheat from Egypt and Africa could the population of Rome be kept quiet. The importance of the wheat-ships can be seen from the references to them in the Acts; St. Paul continued and completed his voyage on Alexandrian ships carrying this cargo to Italy. One of the plans of the Jews who revolted against Rome in the time of Nero was to interfere with this trade and thus rouse the Roman proletariat against the imperial government. The importance of these cargoes is also evident from the fact that the emperors most mindful of their duty to the capital improved its harbour facilities by developing the port of Ostia at the mouth of the Tiber. Reproduced here is a mosaic of the third century found at Ostia; it shows two ships being unloaded in the port. It is the stopping of such supplies that is envisaged in the verse above.

AND he treadeth the winepress of the fierceness and
wrath of Almighty God. (Rev. 19 : 15)

The treading of the winepress as an image of the wrath of God occurs
in the prophecy of Isaiah (see Vol. 6, p. 89); the red of the grape-juice
calls to mind the colour of blood, and the pulping of the grapes
symbolizes the fate of those who oppose the will of the Deity. To the
representations of the winepress from Egypt, reproduced in the
previous volumes, we can here add another from a relief found near
Venice. It shows two labourers holding hands and leaning on sticks;
they are rhythmically jumping in a vat filled with grapes. A third
man on the left is bringing more grapes for the winepress. In the
Roman period more and more use was made of mechanical presses,
but these were in appearance far less picturesque than the primitive
method shown here.

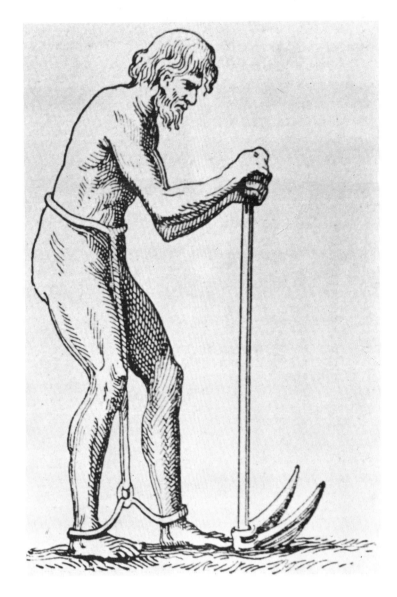

AND I saw an angel come down from heaven, having the key of the bottomless pit and a great chain in his hand.

(Rev. 20 : 1)

After the destruction of the wicked and the overthrow of Rome, the great temporal adversary of God, the time shall come to inaugurate the thousand years of the second reign of Christ on earth by chaining and locking up the power of evil, the great dragon which is the Devil and Satan. The locking up is done with a key, the key of the bottomless pit. Roman keys have been recovered in large numbers; the example shown on the right above was found in one of the caves near the Dead Sea, among the booty carried there by the last remnants of the armies of Bar Kokhba (see V. 12 : 75). The way in which such a key worked can be seen in Vol. 4, p. 18. The protruding studs of the key fitted into corresponding holes in the bolt and lifted the pins which kept the bolt in the locked position; the bolt could then be withdrawn and the door opened. The locking operation, as here, reversed the process. The chain which was brought by the angel for the binding of the dragon corresponded to the ordinary Roman chains found in large numbers wherever there were slaves to be kept bound, as in the illustration on the left. The chaining of the dragon and the locking of the pit indicate the necessity of taking double precautions to prevent the forces of evil from breaking out and wrecking the millennium.

AND had a wall great and high, and had twelve gates... (Rev. 21 : 12)

With the final elimination of Evil, the time has come for a complete regeneration of the universe; a new heaven and a new earth appear, and the Holy City of Jerusalem, which has waited in heaven for this time, comes down on earth to take the place of the sinful city which had been punished by the abomination of desolation (see V.12:67). This concept of a Heavenly Jerusalem as opposed to the earth-bound city is common to both the rabbinical sources and to early Christianity. We find a pictorial representation of Heavenly Jerusalem in the frescoes of the synagogue of Dura Europus (see the illustration). The artist actually intended to depict the Temple of Solomon standing in the middle of the earthly city; but he has encircled the latter with the seven walls of the celestial Jerusalem, each in a different colour. The Temple, in the form of a Hellenistic sanctuary, stands in the middle of the city. The three gates of Jerusalem are adorned with various images of pagan character, such as could be seen on the gates and temples of the cities of the period. Such details, so far from seeming incongruous with the general conception of the Heavenly City, served only to augment its splendour.

He which testifieth these saith, Surely I come quickly; Amen. Even so, come, LORD JESUS. The grace of our LORD JESUS CHRIST be with you all. Amen. (Rev. 22 : 20-21)

The Book of Revelation ends with the solemn assurance that the things described therein would quickly and surely come to pass, and with a blessing to all the faithful. Although the expectation of the return of Christ in the near future and the imminent end of the world was a powerful factor in winning converts for the new faith, it was disparaged by the Church authorities, and above all by St. Paul in his epistles to the Thessalonians. The concluding illustration is taken from the last page of one of the earliest manuscripts of the Greek Bible, the Codex Sinaiticus (fourth cent. A.D.).

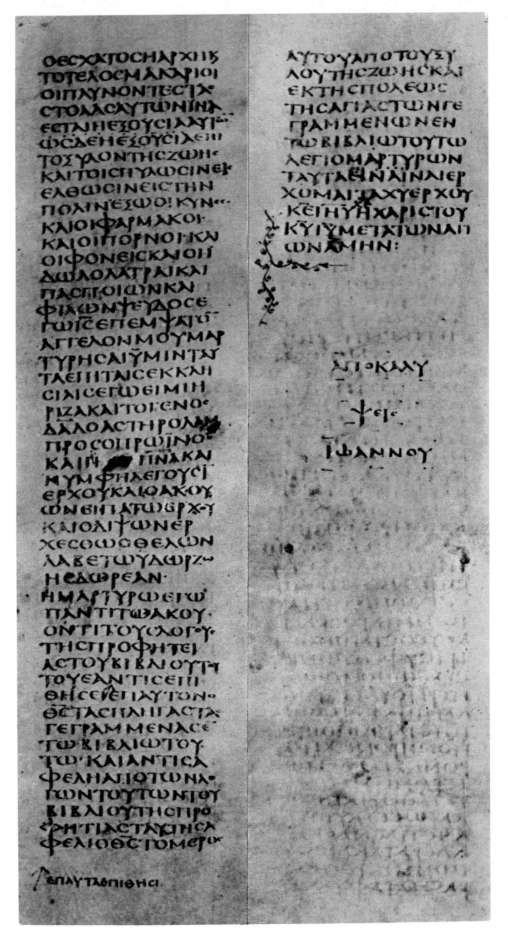

FAMILY BIBLE
REFERENCE
SECTION

· W - X - Y - Z ·

A HOME LIBRARY OF MEMORABLE BIBLE QUOTATIONS

BIOGRAPHIES OF HUNDREDS OF THE MEN AND WOMEN OF THE BIBLE

A CONCISE DICTIONARY OF THE BIBLE—ITS PEOPLE, PLACES, CUSTOMS

AN INTERFAITH GUIDE TO THE HOLY SCRIPTURES

PREFACE

☐ This final volume of THE ILLUSTRATED FAMILY ENCYCLOPEDIA OF THE LIVING BIBLE contains Family Bible Reference Section *W-X-Y-Z*. In it, as before, you will find, alphabetically arranged, a convenient, authoritative selection of Bible quotations, biographies of famous men and women in the Bible, and many more articles on various biblical subjects.

☐ Among the group of quotations, all taken from THE HOME BOOK OF BIBLE QUOTA-TIONS edited by Burton Stevenson (Harper & Row), are *War, Wickedness, Wife, Wisdom, Woman, Word, Work* and *World*.

☐ Brief biographies from THE HANDBOOK OF BIBLICAL PERSONALITIES by George M. Alexander (Seabury Press) include *The Witch of Endor, Zacchaeus, Zechariah, Zedekiah* and *Zephaniah*.

☐ And from DICTIONARY OF THE BIBLE by John L. McKenzie, S.J. (Bruce Bublishing Company) we have excerpted articles on such interesting topics as *War, Water, Wealth, Widow, Wine, Woman* and *World*.

☐ All of these entries have been carefully selected and edited in the hope that they will prove of interest and lasting value to all readers of every faith.

—The Editors

· W ·

WAGES–

Your father hath deceived me, and changed my wages ten times.
— Old Testament: Genesis 31:7, 41

Take this child away, and nurse it for me, and I will give thee thy wages.
— Old Testament: Exodus 2:9

The wages of him that is hired shall not abide with thee all night until this morning.
— Old Testament: Leviticus 19:13

I will be a swift witness against . . . those that oppress the hireling in his wages.
— Old Testament: Malachi 3:5

Be content with your wages.
— New Testament: Luke 3:14

John Baptist to the soldiers who asked his advice.

The wages of sin is death.
— New Testament: Romans 6:23

I robbed other churches, taking wages of them, to do you service.
— New Testament: II Corinthians 11:8

[He] loved the wages of unrighteousness.
— New Testament: II Peter 2:15
(HBBQ)*

WAILING–

They shall weep for thee with . . . bitter wailing.
— Old Testament: Ezekiel 27:31

Wailing shall be in all streets; and they shall say in all the highways, Alas! alas! and they shall call . . . such as are skilful of lamentation to wailing. And in all vineyards shall be wailing.
— Old Testament: Amos 5:16–17

There shall be weeping and gnashing of teeth.
— New Testament: Matthew 8:12; 22:13;
24:51; 25:30; Luke 13:28
(HBBQ)

WAITING–

All the days of my appointed time will I wait.
— Old Testament: Job 14:14

Those that wait upon the Lord, they shall inherit the earth.
— Old Testament: Psalms 37:9

They that wait upon the Lord shall renew their strength.
— Old Testament: Isaiah 40:31

"Wait upon the Lord" is repeated many times.

Wait patiently. . . . I waited patiently.
— Old Testament: Psalms 37:7; 40:1

Blessed are they that wait.
— Old Testament: Isaiah 30:18
(HBBQ)

WALKING–

Ye shall walk in all the ways which the Lord your God hath commanded you.
— Old Testament: Deuteronomy 5:33

[They] walk with stretched forth necks and wanton eyes, walking and mincing as they go, and making a tinkling with their feet.
— Old Testament: Isaiah 3:16

Walk while ye have the light, lest darkness come upon you: for he that walketh in darkness knoweth not whither he goeth.
— New Testament: John 12:35
(HBBQ)

WANT–

A place where there is no want of any thing that is in the earth.
— Old Testament: Judges 18:10; 19:19

The Lord is my shepherd, I shall not want.
— Old Testament: Psalms 23:1

They that seek the Lord shall not want any good thing.
— Old Testament: Psalms 34:10

He that giveth to the rich shall surely come to want.
— Old Testament: Proverbs 22:16

Your abundance may be a supply for their want, and their abundance also may be a supply for your want.
— New Testament: II Corinthians 8:14
(HBBQ)

* The designation (HBBQ) indicates material taken from THE HOME BOOK OF BIBLE QUOTATIONS; (DB) signifies the DICTIONARY OF THE BIBLE; and (HBP) is THE HANDBOOK OF BIBLICAL PERSONALITIES (see PREFACE).

WAR–

The people repent when they see war.
>—Old Testament: Exodus 8:17

All the generation of the men of war were wasted.
>—Old Testament: Deuteronomy 2:14, 16;
>Joshua 5:4, 6

"Men of war" is frequently repeated.

If ye go to war, . . . ye shall blow an alarm with the trumpets.
>—Old Testament: Numbers 10:9

Go armed before the Lord to war.
>—Old Testament: Numbers 22:20

"Go to war" is frequently repeated.

They . . . are gone down to hell with their weapons of war.
>—Old Testament: Ezekiel 32:27

He maketh wars to cease unto the end of the earth; he breaketh the bow, and cutteth the spear in sunder; he burneth the chariot in the fire.
>—Old Testament: Psalms 46:9

Nation shall not lift up sword against nation, neither shall they learn war any more.
>—Old Testament: Isaiah 2:4

Expert in war.
>—Old Testament: I Chronicles 12:33, 35, 36

Let the mighty men come forth; the Ethiopians and the Libyans, that handle the shield; and the Lydians, that handle and bend the bow.
>—Old Testament: Jeremiah 46:9

He teacheth my hands to war.
>—Old Testament: Psalms 18:34

With good advice make war.
>—Old Testament: Proverbs 20:18

They fled from the swords, from the drawn sword, and from the bent bow, and from the grievousness of war.
>—Old Testament: Isaiah 21:15

They that war against thee shall be as nothing.
>—Old Testament: Isaiah 41:12

Ye shall hear of wars and rumors of wars.
>—New Testament: Matthew 24:6; Mark 13:7

What king, going to make war against another king, sitteth not down first, and consulteth whether he be able with ten thousand to meet him that cometh against him with twenty thousand?
>—New Tesament: Luke 14:31

No man that warreth entangleth himself with the affairs of this life; that he may please him who hath chosen him to be a soldier.
>—New Testament: II Timothy 2:4

From whence come wars and fightings among you? come they not hence, even of your lusts that war in your members? . . . Ye fight and war, yet ye have not, because ye ask not.
>—New Testament: James 4:1–2

If it will make no peace with thee, but will make war against thee, then thou shalt besiege it: And when the Lord thy God hath delivered it into thine hands, thou shalt smite every male thereof with the edge of the sword: But the women, and the little ones, and the cattle, and all that is in the city, even all the spoil thereof, shalt thou take unto thyself.
>—Old Testament: Deuteronomy 20:12–14

There is . . . a time of war, and a time of peace.
>—Old Testament: Ecclesiastes 3:8
>(HBBQ)

War was a normal state in the ancient world of the Near East; there are few years of record without campaigning. The ancient war was a candid war of conquest or looting. Both of these ends were sanctified by the religious character of war, which was fought on behalf of the gods of the people and under the leadership and protection of the gods. The cruelty and barbarism of ancient war were equally candid; ancient war is shocking only because it involved the primitive means of personal effort, and could not achieve the vast mechanical horrors of modern warfare. Prisoners of war had no rights whatever; the entire population could be enslaved, unless the defeated enemy were regarded as a menace to the victor; if it were, the male population could be exterminated or mutilated. Destruction of conquered towns was a normal act of the victor.

The time for beginning a campaign was the spring, which afforded at least six months of movement before the rainy season. War could not be carried on actively in the winter. . . . The ancient battle was often no more than a melee of confused fighting; indeed, it could be no more than a rush of two shouting groups toward each other until one group yielded to panic; after that the battle was flight and slaughter. . . . The more successful warring nations of the ancient world, however, knew the importance of discipline and mass movement. The armies used projectiles before they came to close quarters, and preferred to keep close ranks and force their way with pikes rather than permit the attack to degenerate into private quarrels. Ancient sources refer several times to a complete loss of discipline when victory was achieved and the camp or city of the enemy was open to plunder. The infantry column was the backbone of offensive war; the chariot was useful only on open ground, and mounted men, a relatively late military innovation, annoyed infantry rather than harmed it. The ancient commanders knew the importance of fortified positions which made the attacker come up to them. Strategy included such deceptions as the ambush, and the division of forces for an attack in the rear or a pincer movement. The defenders preferred strong entrenchments, but techniques to force them were successful if handled with determination. Espionage or scouting of the enemy's strength before attack was used. It is not clear that ancient Near Eastern warfare included the single combat of champions such as the combats described in Homer, and which were the main events of medieval warfare until the battle of Crécy. Such combats are reported of David and Goliath and at the battle of Joab and Abner at Gibeon; but here possibly Mycenean practices had been introduced through the Philistines.

In Israel, at least until the monarchy, war was the holy war. The wars of Israel were the wars of Yahweh. . . . The technical phrase for initiating war was to "sanctify" war and warriors, i.e., to place them in a state of holiness for holy activity. It seems probable that this consecration included abstinence from sexual activity. Yahweh was present in the camp through the symbolic presence of the ark; it does not appear that the ark was still carried into war after Solomon. A motto of Israel was "Yahweh is my standard [of war]". . . . The priestly ideal of a sacred war is set forth in the midrash of Numbers 31: the fulfillment of all the prescribed ritual and the ban upon the prisoners and the booty. The law of war of Deuteronomy 20 is another and earlier rationalization of war; it is an effort to make it more humane both in its demands upon the combatants and in the treatment of conquered enemies, but it retains the ideal of the ban for Canaanites. The law possibly reflects the change in the character of war from the holy war of the tribal confederacy to the organized political wars of the monarchy. The change in the

concept of war was merely a reflection of the change in the state and the change in the composition of the army. The state was now the king; the army was still the levy of Israel, the host, but its nucleus was a corps of professional soldiers who were the personal guard of the king. The frequency of war has filled the Bible with metaphors drawn from war which are too numerous to cite.

Modern readers find the Israelite concept of the holy war a primitive type of morality; this it is, but it is doubtfully more primitive than the modern concept of war. Where the Bible relates the thought patterns of early Israel, it does not seem to rise above the thought of its time; and its conception of Yahweh as a warrior was an imperfect apprehension of His reality and activity. The Bible itself presents the elements which permit man to emancipate himself from the idea of war, which is primitive in ancient or modern times. Several passages of the prophets expressly renounce war as a means of the salvation of Israel. . . . The prophets assert that the military means by which Israel thinks to escape judgment are sure to fail; not their security, but their mere survival is assured only by faith. . . . Presumably they would approve war as a national policy only if a nation were not under the judgment of Yahweh.

The New Testament takes no different position, although it is not explicit; since the early Christian community was not a political society and had no part in determining policy, the question did not arise as it did for the prophets. Soldiers pass through the New Testament and their calling is not noticed except that John the Baptist warned them not to abuse their power (Luke 3:14). The saying of Jesus concerning the sword is relevant (Matthew 26:52); Jesus seems to have no expectation of abolishing war, but He affirms that it destroys those who engage in it. Warfare appears frequently in metaphors which describe the Christian life or illustrate the preaching of the gospel; Jesus uses it in parables (Matthew 22:7; Luke 11:17; 14:31 f.), Paul alludes to military service to illustrate the apostolate (I Corinthians 9:7) and to the trumpet which summons to war (I Corinthians 14:8). . . .

The eschatological judgment is described as a war both in Old Testament and New Testament. . . . The theme of the eschatological war is much

The designation (HBBQ) indicates material taken from THE HOME BOOK OF BIBLE QUOTATIONS; (DB) signifies the DICTIONARY OF THE BIBLE; and (HBP) is THE HANDBOOK OF BIBLICAL PERSONALITIES.

more prominent in the apocryphal literature, which is now supplemented by the Qumran scroll of the war of the sons of light against the sons of darkness. A striking difference between the Qumran conception and the biblical conception is that in the biblical conception the hostile forces are scattered by the power of God or by angelic forces; in Qumran it is a combat between two groups of men. The sons of light, of course, win a miraculously certain and easy victory by the power of God, but they are the active combatants. In the New Testament the imagery of the apocalyptic war appears only in Apocalypse 12:7, the war between the angels led by Michael and the dragon, and Apocalypse 20:9, where the forces of the dragon are annihilated in their final attack by the power of God.

(DB)*

WATCHING–

In our watching we have watched for a nation that could not save us.
—Old Testament: Lamentations 4:17

Go, and ye shall receive: . . . the kingdom is already prepared for you: watch.
—Old Testament Apocrypha: II Esdras 2:13

Watch therefore: for ye know not what hour your Lord doth come.
—New Testament: Matthew 24:42; 25:13

Take ye heed, watch and pray. . . . What I say unto you I say unto all, Watch.
—New Testament: Mark 13:33–37

Watch and pray, that ye enter not into temptation.
—New Testament: Matthew 26:41; Mark 14:38

Watch ye therefore, and pray always.
—New Testament: Luke 21:36; Acts 20:31; I Corinthians 16:13; Colossians 4:2

Let us not sleep as do others; but let us watch and be sober.
—New Testament: I Thessalonians 5:6

Be ye therefore sober, and watch unto prayer.
—New Testament: I Peter 4:7

Blessed is he that watcheth.
—New Testament: Revelation 16:15

Then Jesus . . . saith unto the disciples, . . . Tarry ye here and watch with me.
—New Testament: Matthew 26:38; Mark 14:34

Except the Lord keep the city, the watchman waketh but in vain.
—Old Testament: Psalms 127:1

Watchman, what of the night? Watchman, what of the night?
—Old Testament: Isaiah 21:11

His watchmen are blind: they are all ignorant, they are all dumb dogs, they cannot bark; sleeping, lying down, loving to slumber. Yea, they are greedy dogs which can never have enough.
—Old Testament: Isaiah 56:10–11

Watchers come from a far country.
—Old Testament: Jeremiah 4:16

The king saw a watcher . . . coming down from heaven.
—Old Testament: Daniel 4:23
(HBBQ)

WATER–

Give me, I pray thee, a little water of thy pitcher to drink.
—Old Testament: Genesis 24:43; Judges 4:19

Unstable as water, thou shalt not excel.
—Old Testament: Genesis 49:4

A water of separation: it is a purification for sin.
—Old Testament: Numbers 19:9, 13, 20, 21

And there was no water for the congregation: and they gathered themselves together against Moses and against Aaron. . . . And the Lord spake unto Moses, saying, Take the rod, . . . and speak ye unto the rock before their eyes; and it shall give forth his water, and thou shalt bring forth to them water out of the rock. . . . And Moses took the rod, . . . and lifted up his hand, and with his rod he smote the rock twice: and the water came out abundantly, and congregation drank, and their beasts also.
—Old Testament: Numbers 20:2–11

I give waters in the wilderness, and rivers in the desert, to give drink to my people, my chosen.
—Old Testament: Isaiah 43:20

Ye shall not see wind, neither shall ye see rain: yet that valley shall be filled with water, that ye may drink, both ye, and your cattle, and your beasts.
—Old Testament: II Kings 3:17

I will pour water upon him that is thirsty.
—Old Testament: Isaiah 44:3

Water will quench a flaming fire.
—Old Testament: Ecclesiasticus 3:30

He walked on the water.
—New Testament: Matthew 14:29

The water that was made wine.
—New Testament: John 2:9

Whosoever drinketh of the water that I shall give him shall never thirst; but the water that I shall give him shall be in him a well of water springing up into everlasting life. The woman saith unto him, Sir, give me this water, that I thirst not.
—New Testament: John 4:14–15 (HBBQ)

The average rainfall of Palestine is sufficient to support agriculture; but the country lacks rivers, perennial streams, and lakes and is more arid than Europe or most of North America. Furthermore, the steppes and the desert lie close to Palestine proper. Hence the Bible exhibits an awareness of the meaning of water for life and of the dire consequences which follow when it falls. The imagery of the Bible is rich in symbols drawn from water. Water is secured from springs and wells or by preserving rain water in cisterns. The Bible mentions a number of pools connected with towns: Gibeon, Hebron, Samaria, Jerusalem. Archaeology has uncovered a number of complex hydraulic installations for channeling and storing water both from springs or wells and from rainfall. Water was sold on the streets of ancient Jerusalem, as it is in modern Near Eastern cities. Water rights were often the occasion of bickering, but they could be obtained by payment. Rare as water might be, courtesy demanded that a drink be offered to the thirsty traveler, even if it had to be drawn from a deep well. The refreshing quality of water is not unworthy of the Israelite poet (Psalms 23:3; 42:2; Proverbs 25:25). "Living water," which is water from a well or spring or stream, is preferred to the water of pools and cisterns. The drawing of water is the work of women, and this can still be seen in the towns and villages of the Near East; it is this which gives point to Jesus' direction that His disciples should look for a man carrying a vessel of water (Luke 22:10). Water is used in religious ablutions; it is the element of the basic Christian initiation of baptism, in which almost its entire symbolism appears. . . . Water is the primordial element (Genesis 1:2); it is not enumerated among the works of creation, but is presupposed. In the Paradise story the growth of vegetation begins with the flow of the four rivers of Paradise. It may be asked whether the story of the drawing of Moses from the water (Exodus 2:3–10) may not be composed to present to him the symbolic saving which he later brings to Israel. The might of Yahweh in saving Israel appears in His power over water; He corrupts water, the life of Egypt, and divides the water through which Israel survives and in which the Egyptians perish (Exodus 14:21–30). . . .

(DB)

WATERS–

The Spirit of God moved upon the face of the waters.
—Old Testament: Genesis 1:2

And God said, Let there be a firmament in the midst of the waters, and let it divide the waters from the waters. And God . . . divided the waters which were under the firmament from the waters which were above the firmament: and it was so.
—Old Testament: Genesis 1:6–7

And God said, Let the waters under the heaven be gathered together unto one place. . . . And the gathering together of the waters called he Seas.
—Old Testament: Genesis 1:9–10

And God said, Let the waters bring forth abundantly the moving creature that hath life.
—Old Testament: Genesis 1:20

I, even I, do bring a flood of waters upon the earth.
—Old Testament: Genesis 6:17

Waters shall no more become a flood to destroy all flesh.
—Old Testament: Genesis 9:15

Behold, he withholdeth the waters, and they dry up: also he sendeth them out, and they overturn the earth.
—Old Testament: Job 12:15

He leadeth me beside the still waters.
—Old Testament: Psalms 23:2

I am come into deep waters, where the floods overflow me. . . . Let me be delivered . . . out of the deep waters.
—Old Testament: Psalms 69:2, 14

Stolen waters are sweet.
—Old Testament: Proverbs 9:17

The waters shall fail from the sea, and the river shall be wasted and dried up.
—Old Testament: Isaiah 19:5

The designation (HBBQ) indicates material taken from THE HOME BOOK OF BIBLE QUOTATIONS; (DB) signifies the DICTIONARY OF THE BIBLE; and (HBP) is THE HANDBOOK OF BIBLICAL PERSONALITIES.

In the wilderness shall waters break out. . . . And the parched ground shall become a pool, and the thirsty land springs of water.
—Old Testament: Isaiah 35:6–7

When thou passest through the waters, I will be with thee; and through the rivers, they shall not overflow thee.
—Old Testament: Isaiah 43:2

Then will I make their waters deep, and cause their rivers to run like oil, saith the Lord.
—Old Testament: Ezekiel 32:14
(HBBQ)

WAY–

They shall keep the way of the Lord.
—Old Testament: Genesis 18:19

[He] went on his way rejoicing.
—New Testament: Acts 8:39

Shew me now thy way, that I may know thee.
—Old Testament: Exodus 33:13

Teach them the good way wherein they should walk.
—Old Testament: I Kings 8:36

By the way that he came, by the same shall he return.
—Old Testament: II Kings 19:33; Isaiah 37:34

Let their way be dark and slippery.
—Old Testament: Psalms 35:6

I hate every false way.
—Old Testament: Psalms 119:104, 128

I lead in the way of righteousness.
—Old Testament: Proverbs 8:20; 12:28; 15:19

The way of the wicked is an abomination unto the Lord.
—Old Testament: Proverbs 15:9

Prepare ye the way of the Lord.
—New Testament: Matthew 3:3;
Mark 1:3; Luke 3:4

Make straight the way of the Lord.
—New Testament: John 1:23

Guide our feet into the way of peace.
—New Testament: Luke 1:79

Shew unto us the way of salvation.
—New Testament: Acts 16:17

Jesus saith unto him, I am the way, the truth, and the life.
—New Testament: John 14:6

Ye shall walk in all the ways which the Lord your God hath commanded you.
—Old Testament: Deuteronomy 5:33; 8:6;
10:12; 11:22; 19:9; 26:27, etc., etc.

Shew me thy ways, O Lord; teach me thy paths.
—Old Testament: Psalms 25:4

Neither are your ways my ways, saith the Lord. For as the heavens are higher than the earth, so are my ways higher than your ways.
—Old Testament: Isaiah 55:8–9

Make your ways and your doings good.
—Old Testament: Jeremiah 18:11

Let them turn every one from his evil ways.
—Old Testament: Jonah 3:8, 10; Zechariah 1:4

The rough ways shall be made smooth.
—New Testament: Luke 3:5
(HBBQ)

WEAKNESS–

Have mercy upon me, O Lord; for I am weak.
—Old Testament: Psalms 6:2

To the weak became I as weak, that I might gain the weak.
—New Testament: I Corinthians 9:22

The weakness of God is stronger than men.
—New Testament: I Corinthians 1:25

He was crucified through weakness.
—New Testament: II Corinthians 13:4

Out of weakness [they] were made strong.
—New Testament: Hebrews 11:34
(HBBQ)

WEALTH–

They that trust in their wealth, . . . None of them can by any means redeem his brother.
—Old Testament: Psalms 49:6

Wise men die, likewise the fool and the brutish person perish, and leave their wealth to others.
—Old Testament: Psalms 49:10

The rich man's wealth is his strong city.
—Old Testament: Proverbs 10:15; 18:11

Wealth gotten by vanity shall be diminished: but he that gathereth by labor shall increase.
—Old Testament: Proverbs 13:11

Let no man seek his own, but every man another's wealth.
—New Testament: I Corinthians 10:24
(HBBQ)

1. *Old Testament.* In the older books of the Old Testament no definite attitude toward wealth appears; it is simply a gift of Yahweh. In early Israel wealth was not a social or moral problem; no one acquired great wealth and a minority group of the wealthy in opposition to the mass of the poor had not yet arisen. Even after the social division of rich and poor which developed under the monarchy the criticism of the prophets dealt more with the protection of the poor than with the rich as a distinct class. There is, however, a steady refrain of charges against the rich that they oppress the poor, exact debts without mercy, and drive the poor into enslavement, which carries the implication that no one could acquire and retain great wealth except by dishonest means. Both Isaiah (3:16; 4:1) and Amos (5:8–10) speak of the wives of the wealthy who by their demands for luxury impel their husbands to acquire wealth by dishonest actions. These texts indicate the existence of a small class of wealthy who were greedy and rapacious and who were utterly unscrupulous in their business. The existence of this class was a weakness of the social fabric of Israel and a solvent of the ancient unity of clan and tribe derived from the nomadic past of early Israel. The class arose under the monarchy and under its patronage, and very probably had its origin in the officers of the court, whose position gave them opportunities to amass wealth.

The wisdom literature exhibits an ambivalent attitude toward wealth. At times wealth is praised and admired. . . . More frequently wealth is viewed unfavorably. Sirach draws a number of antitheses between the rich and the poor which are not laudatory of the rich. The rich man does wrong and adds a threat, while the poor must apologize when he is wronged. When the rich man falls, there are many to help him; when he speaks, all are silent. When the rich man rests from his toil to amass wealth he enjoys luxury; if the poor man rests, he becomes destitute. Wealth and poverty are not adequate criteria of a man's worth; the rich man is honored for his wealth, the poor for his knowledge. The rich is wise in his own eyes, and an intelligent poor man tests him. Who trusts in his riches will fail. . . .

These and other examples of wisdom literature are instances of "the piety of the poor." To some extent they reflect the effort of the sages to find contentment in poverty by reflections on the disadvantages of wealth, its temptations, and the moral obliquity which in the ancient world seemed a prerequisite for the acquisition of wealth. The sayings of the wise are echoed in some passages of the New Testament.

2. *New Testament.* The words of Jesus Himself are more frequently directed to a positive approach toward poverty than to a negative criticism of wealth. The classic text for wealth and poverty is the parable of the rich man who rejected the invitation of Jesus to follow Him (Matthew 19:16–30; Mark 10:17–31; Luke 18:18–30). The episode elicits the sayings about the difficulty which the rich have in entering the kingdom of heaven, compared to the passage of a camel through the eye of a needle. While this saying contains hyperbole, it can scarcely mean anything but moral impossibility; Jesus makes wealth an insuperable obstacle to salvation, and offers no solution of the difficulty except that one should give away one's riches. Attempts to rationalize this saying into something else have no success. Jesus also draws a comparison between the contributions of the rich to the temple and the contribution of an impoverished widow (Mark 12:41–44; Luke 21:1–4). The gift which does not actually deprive the giver of something but comes from his superfluity is of no account. A striking contrast between the extremes of wealth and poverty is presented in the parable of Dives and Lazarus (Luke 16:19–31); the sin of Dives consists in no more than living in luxury while dire poverty is near. The passages in which Jesus speaks of wealth are few, but they do not lack strength of language.

(DB)

WEARINESS–

I am weary of my life.
——Old Testament: Genesis 27:46

Thou wast faint and weary.
——Old Testament: Deuteronomy 25:18

Thou art wearied in the greatness of thy way.
——Old Testament: Isaiah 57:10

The designation (HBBQ) indicates material taken from THE HOME BOOK OF BIBLE QUOTATIONS; (DB) signifies the DICTIONARY OF THE BIBLE; and (HBP) is THE HANDBOOK OF BIBLICAL PERSONALITIES.

Is it a small thing for you to weary men, but will ye weary my God also?
—Old Testament: Isaiah 7:13

Be not weary: for when the day of trouble and heaviness cometh others shall weep and be sorrowful, but thou shalt be merry and have abundance.
Old Testament Apocrypha: II Esdras 2:27

Let us not be weary in well doing.
—New Testament: Galatians 6:9
(HBBQ)

WEEPING–

She sat over against him, and lift up her voice, and wept.
—Old Testament: Genesis 21:16

They wept one with another.
—Old Testament: I Samuel 20:41

And David went up by the ascent of mount Olivet, and wept as he went up, and had his head covered, and he went barefoot: and all the people that was with him covered every man his head, and they went up, weeping as they went up.
—Old Testament: II Samuel 15:30

Weeping may endure for a night, but joy cometh in the morning.
—Old Testament: Psalms 30:5

He that goeth forth and weepeth, bearing precious seed, shall doubtless come again with rejoicing, bringing his sheaves with him.
—Old Testament: Psalms 126:6

A time to weep, and a time to laugh.
—Old Testament: Ecclesiastes 3:4

Blessed are ye that weep now: for ye shall laugh. . . . Woe unto you that laugh now! for ye shall mourn and weep.
—New Testament: Luke 6:21, 25

I will weep bitterly, labor not to comfort me.
—Old Testament: Isaiah 22:4

He went out, and wept bitterly.
—New Testament: Matthew 26:75; Luke 22:62

Thou shalt weep no more.
—Old Testament: Isaiah 30:19

Oh . . . that I might weep day and night.
—Old Testament: Jeremiah 9:1

My soul shall weep in secret places, . . . and mine eye shall weep sore.
—Old Testament: Jeremiah 13:17

Fail not to be with them that weep.
—Old Testament Apocrypha: Ecclesiasticus 7:34

Rejoice with them that do rejoice, and weep with them that weep.
—New Testament: Romans 12:15

Many shall come from the east and west, and shall sit down with Abraham, and Isaac, and Jacob, in the kingdom of heaven. But the children of the kingdom shall be cast out into outer darkness; there shall be weeping and gnashing of teeth.
—New Testament: Matthew 8:11–12

The last phrase repeated in 22:13; 24:51; 25:30; Luke 13:28.

He had compassion on her, and said unto her, Weep not.
—New Testament: Luke 7:13; 8:52

Weep not for me, but weep for yourselves.
—New Testament: Luke 23:28
(HBBQ)

WHIRLWIND–

Behold, a whirlwind of the Lord is gone forth in fury, even a grievous whirlwind: it shall fall grievously upon the head of the wicked.
—Old Testament: Jeremiah 23:19; 30:23

They shall be . . . as the chaff that is driven with the whirlwind.
—Old Testament: Hosea 13:3

A great whirlwind shall be raised up from the coasts of the earth.
—Old Testament: Jeremiah 25:32

They shall reap the whirlwind.
—Old Testament: Hosea 8:7
(HBBQ)

WHISPER–

All that hate me whisper together against me.
—Old Testament: Psalms 41:7

A whisperer separateth chief friends.
—Old Testament: Proverbs 16:28

A whisperer defileth his own soul, and is hated wheresoever he dwelleth.
—Old Testament Apocrypha: Ecclesiasticus 21:28

Curse the whisperer and doubletongued: for such have destroyed many that were at peace.
—Old Testament Apocrypha: Ecclesiasticus 28:13
(HBBQ)

WHORE–

Do not prostitute thy daughter, to cause her to be a whore; lest the land fall to whoredom.
—Old Testament: Leviticus 19:29

The only use of "prostitute."

She hath wrought folly in Israel, to play the whore in her father's house.
>—Old Testament: Deuteronomy 22:21

By means of a whorish woman a man is brought to a piece of bread.
>—Old Testament: Proverbs 6:26

A whore is a deep ditch; and a strange woman is a narrow pit. She also lieth in wait as for a prey, and increaseth the transgressors among men.
>—Old Testament: Proverbs 23:27–28

A whore envieth a right honest and virtuous woman.
>—Old Testament Apocrypha: II Esdras 16:48

I will shew unto thee the judgment of the great whore that sitteth upon many waters.
>—New Testament: Revelation 17:1

The waters . . . where the whore sitteth are peoples.
>—New Testament: Revelation 17:15

These shall hate the whore, and shall make her desolate and naked.
>—New Testament: Revelation 17:16

He hath judged the great whore, which did corrupt the earth with her fornication.
>—New Testament: Revelation 19:2

These are the only uses of "whore" in the New Testament. The references are to Babylon.

Thou hast polluted the land with thy whoredoms.
>—Old Testament: Jeremiah 3:2

Is this of thy whoredoms a small matter? . . . In all . . . thy whoredoms thou hast not remembered the days of thy youth.
>—Old Testament: Ezekiel 16:20, 22

The whoredom of a woman may be known in her haughty looks and eyelids.
>—Old Testament Apocrypha: Ecclesiasticus 26:9

They go a whoring after their gods. . . . And their daughters go a whoring after their gods, and make thy sons go a whoring.
>—Old Testament: Exodus 34:15–16

I will set my face against that man, . . . and all that go a whoring after him.
>—Old Testament: Leviticus 20:5, 6

They went a whoring after other gods.
>—Old Testament: Judges 2:17;
>I Chronicles 5:25
>(HBBQ)

WICKEDNESS—

I will not justify the wicked.
>—Old Testament: Exodus 23:7

If ye shall still do wickedly, ye shall be consumed.
>—Old Testament: I Samuel 12:25

For the wickedness of these nations the Lord doth drive them out before thee.
>—Old Testament: Deuteronomy 9:4

If there be found among you . . . man or woman, that hath wrought wickedness in the sight of the Lord thy God, . . . Then shalt thou bring forth that man or that woman, . . . and shalt stone them with stones, till they die.
>—Old Testament: Deuteronomy 17:2–5

As saith the proverb of the ancients, Wickedness proceedeth from the wicked.
>—Old Testament: I Samuel 24:13

The eyes of the wicked shall fail, and they shall not escape.
>—Old Testament: Job 11:20

Yea, the light of the wicked shall be put out, and the spark of his fire shall not shine. The light shall be dark in his tabernacle, and his candle shall be put out with him. His own counsel shall cast him down. For he is cast into a net by his own feet. . . . His remembrance shall perish from the earth.
>—Old Testament: Job 18:5–17

Knowest thou not this of old, since man was placed upon earth, That the triumphing of the wicked is short?
>—Old Testament: Job 20:4–5

Let not wickedness dwell in thy tabernacles.
>—Old Testament: Job 11:14

Is not thy wickedness great? . . . For thou hast . . . stripped the naked of their clothing. Thou hast not given water to the weary to drink, and thou hast withholden bread from the hungry. . . . Thou hast sent widows away empty. . . . Therefore snares are round about thee, and sudden fear troubleth thee.
>—Old Testament: Job 22:5–10

Wherefore do the wicked live, become old, yea, are mighty in power? . . . Their houses are safe from fear. . . . They take the timbrel and harp, and rejoice at the sound of the organ. They spend their days in wealth, and in a moment go down to the grave.
>—Old Testament: Job 21:7–13

Tread down the wicked in their place. Hide them in the dust together; and bind their faces in secret.
>—Old Testament: Job 40:12–13

The designation (HBBQ) indicates material taken from THE HOME BOOK OF BIBLE QUOTATIONS; (DB) signifies the DICTIONARY OF THE BIBLE; and (HBP) is THE HANDBOOK OF BIBLICAL PERSONALITIES.

The wicked in his pride doth persecute the poor: let them be taken in the devices that they have imagined. For the wicked boasteth of his heart's desire, and blesseth the covetous, whom the Lord abhorreth. . . . His mouth is full of cursing and deceit and fraud: under his tongue is mischief and vanity. . . . In the secret places doth he murder the innocent.
—Old Testament: Psalms 10:2–8

The wicked plotteth against the just, and gnasheth upon him with his teeth.
—Old Testament: Psalms 37:12

The wicked have drawn out the sword, and have bent their bow, . . . to slay such as be of upright conversation.
—Old Testament: Psalms 37:14

Upon the wicked he shall rain . . . fire and brimstone, and an horrible tempest: this shall be the portion of their cup.
—Old Testament: Psalms 11:6

The seed of the wicked shall be cut off.
—Old Testament: Psalms 37:28

Deliver my soul from the wicked.
—Old Testament: Psalms 17:13

Hide me from the secret council of the wicked. . . . Who whet their tongue like a sword.
—Old Testament: Psalms 64:2–3

Deliver me, O my God, out of the hand of the wicked.
—Old Testament: Psalms 71:4; 140:4

The righteous . . . shall wash his feet in the blood of the wicked. So that a man shall say, Verily there is a reward for the righteous: verily he is a God that judgeth in the earth.
—Old Testament: Psalms 58:10–11

I said . . . to the wicked, Lift not up the horn: Lift not up your horn on high: speak not with a stiff neck. . . . All the horns of the wicked also will I cut off.
—Old Testament: Psalms 75:4–5, 10

"Horns" symbolize strength. "To lift one's horn" is to be arrogant; "to exalt one's horn" is to strengthen or prosper him; "to cut off one's horn" is to crush or weaken him.

Let the wicked be no more.
—Old Testament: Psalms 104:35

The Lord is righteous: he hath cut asunder the cords of the wicked.
—Old Testament: Psalms 129:4

Grant not, O Lord, the desires of the wicked: further not his wicked device; lest they exalt themselves.
—Old Testament: Psalms 140:8

The wicked shall be cut off from the earth.
—Old Testament: Proverbs 2:22

Enter not into the path of the wicked, . . . For they sleep not, except they have done mischief. . . . They eat the bread of wickedness, and drink the wine of violence.
—Old Testament: Proverbs 4:14–17

The way of the wicked is as darkness: they know not at what they stumble.
—Old Testament: Proverbs 4:19

The wicked shall not inhabit the earth.
—Old Testament: Proverbs 10:30

A wicked man is loathsome, and cometh to shame.
—Old Testament: Proverbs 13:5

The Lord is far from the wicked.
—Old Testament: Proverbs 15:29

He that justifieth the wicked, and he that condemneth the just, even they both are abomination to the Lord.
—Old Testament: Proverbs 17:15

It is not good to accept the person of the wicked, to overthrow the righteous in judgment.
—Old Testament: Proverbs 18:5

A wicked man hardeneth his face.
—Old Testament: Proverbs 21:29

The wicked shall fall into mischief.
—Old Testament: Proverbs 24:16

There shall be no reward for the evil man; the candle of the wicked shall be put out.
—Old Testament: Proverbs 24:20

A righteous man falling down before the wicked is as a troubled fountain, and a corrupt spring.
—Old Testament: Proverbs 25:26

The wicked flee when no man pursueth: but the righteous are bold as a lion.
—Old Testament: Proverbs 28:1

All things have I seen in the days of my vanity: there is a just man that perisheth in his righteousness, and there is a wicked man that prolongeth his life in his wickedness.
—Old Testament: Ecclesiastes 7:15

There is a vanity which is done upon the earth; that there be just men unto whom it happeneth according to the work of the wicked; again, there be wicked men, to whom it happeneth according to the work of the righteous: I said that this also is vanity.
—Old Testament: Ecclesiastes 8:14

Woe unto the wicked! it shall be ill with him: for the reward of his hands shall be given him.
—Old Testament: Isaiah 3:11

Thou hast trusted in thy wickedness: thou hast said, None seeth me.
—Old Testament: Isaiah 47:10

There is no peace, saith the Lord, unto the wicked.
—Old Testament: Isaiah 48:22

Let the wicked forsake his way, and the unrighteous man his thoughts: and let him return unto the Lord, and he will have mercy upon him; and to our God, for he will abundantly pardon.
—Old Testament: Isaiah 55:7

Wash thine heart from wickedness, that thou mayest be saved.
—Old Testament: Jeremiah 4:14

As a fountain casteth out her waters, so she casteth out her wickedness.
—Old Testament: Jeremiah 6:7

In my house have I found their wickedness, saith the Lord.
—Old Testament: Jeremiah 23:11

Have ye forgotten the wickedness of your fathers, . . . and your own wickedness, and the wickedness of your wives?
—Old Testament: Jeremiah 44:9

If the wicked will turn from all his sins that he hath committed, and keep all my statutes, and do that which is lawful and right, he shall surely live, he shall not die.
—Old Testament: Ezekiel 18:21; 33:15, 19

Wine is wicked, the king is wicked, women are wicked, all the children of men are wicked, and such are all their wicked works; and there is no truth in them.
—Old Testament Apocrypha: I Esdras 4:37

Whoso taketh pleasure in wickedness shall be condemned: but he that resisteth pleasures crowneth his life.
—Old Testament Apocrypha: Ecclesiasticus 19:5

To depart from wickedness is a thing pleasing to the Lord; and to forsake unrighteousness is a propitiation.
—Old Testament Apocrypha: Ecclesiasticus 35:3

Many are the troubles of the wicked; but they that trust in the Lord, mercy shall encompass them about.
—Old Testament Apocrypha: I Clement 11:8

Put away from among yourselves that wicked person.
—New Testament: I Corinthians 5:13

Pray . . . that we may be delivered from unreasonable and wicked men.
—New Testament: II Thessalonians 3:2
(HBBQ)

WIDOW—

Ye shall not afflict any widow, or fatherless child. If thou afflict them in any wise, and they cry at all unto me, I will surely hear their cry; And my wrath shall wax hot, and I will kill you with the sword; and your wives shall be widows, and your children fatherless.
—Old Testament: Exodus 22:22–24

The Lord your God . . . doth execute the judgment of the fatherless and widow.
—Old Testament: Deuteronomy 10:18

Thou shalt not . . . take a widow's raiment to pledge.
—Old Testament: Deuteronomy 24:17

When thou cuttest down thine harvest in thy field, and hast forgot a sheaf in the field, thou shalt not go again to fetch it: it shall be for the stranger, for the fatherless, and for the widow.
—Old Testament: Deuteronomy 24:19, 20, 21; 26:12, 13

I am indeed a widow woman, and mine husband is dead.
—Old Testament: II Samuel 14:5

The phrase, "A widow woman," is repeated in I Kings 11:26; 17:9, 10.

His widows shall not weep.
—Old Testament: Job 27:15

I caused the widow's heart to sing for joy.
—Old Testament: Job 29:13

A judge of the widows, is God in his holy habitation.
—Old Testament: Psalms 68:5

Learn to do well; . . . plead for the widow.
—Old Testament: Isaiah 1:17

Thou sayest in thine heart, . . . I shall not sit as a widow, neither shall I know the loss of children: But these two things shall come to thee in a moment in one day, the loss of children, and widowhood.
—Old Testament: Isaiah 47:8–9

Oppress not . . . the widow.
—Old Testament: Jeremiah 7:6; Zechariah 7:10

Do no wrong, do no violence to the stranger, the fatherless, nor the widow.
—Old Testament: Jeremiah 22:3

Let us not spare the widow.
—Old Testament Apocrypha: Wisdom of Solomon 2:10

The designation (HBBQ) indicates material taken from THE HOME BOOK OF BIBLE QUOTATIONS; (DB) signifies the DICTIONARY OF THE BIBLE; and (HBP) is THE HANDBOOK OF BIBLICAL PERSONALITIES.

Now she that is a widow indeed, and desolate, trusteth in God, and continueth in supplications and prayers night and day. But she that liveth in pleasure is dead while she liveth.

New Testament: I Timothy 5:5–6
(HBBQ)

In ancient society the independent woman did not exist; she was a member of a family and dependent upon her father or upon her husband. The position of a widow could therefore be difficult. . . . She could not inherit from her husband, and in the early period she was a part of the inheritance of the eldest son. If she was childless she returned to her father's house. She could marry again, although priests were not allowed to marry widows unless they were widows of priests. The woman who had no man to defend her rights was an obvious victim for the exactions of a creditor and for any type of oppression; the "murder" of widows in Psalms 94:6 may be a hyperbole, except that exactions and dishonest oppression could reduce the widow to starvation. The widow had no defender at law and was therefore at the mercy of dishonest judges. Israelite law extended protection to them by prohibiting injustice in the cases of widows, including a curse upon injustice (Deuteronomy 27:19); but the allusions elsewhere in the Old Testament show that such a general law with no practical implementation was a lifeless ideal. . . .
The primitive Church made the practical care of its widows a concern. It provided food for them and Dorcas is praised because she made clothing for widows (Acts 9:39). Care of widows and orphans is one of the two elements of genuine religion mentioned in James 1:27. It is indicated in I Timothy 5:3–16 that the care of widows had become well organized. There was an approved list of widows who might receive care from the Church. They had to be 60 years of age and childless; if they had relatives, their care fell upon the relatives and the Church would not substitute. The accepted widow must have established a reputation of good life and was expected to devote herself entirely to prayer and good works. The animus of the writer against younger widows is severe and it is hard to see how he expected them to be supported, if they were in straits, except by a second marriage.

(DB)

WIFE–

Therefore shall a man leave his father and his mother, and shall cleave unto his wife: and they shall be one flesh.

—Old Testament: Genesis 2:24

The Pharisees also came unto him [Jesus], tempting him, and saying unto him, Is it lawful for a man to put away his wife for every cause? And he answered and said unto them, Have ye not read, that he which made them at the beginning made them male and female, And said, For this cause shall a man leave father and mother, and shall cleave to his wife: and they twain shall be one flesh? Wherefore they are no more twain, but one flesh. What therefore God hath joined together, let not man put asunder.

—New Testament: Matthew 19:3–6

From the beginning of the creation God made them male and female. For this cause shall a man leave his father and mother, and cleave to his wife; And they twain shall be one flesh: so then they are no more twain, but one flesh. What therefore God hath joined together, let not man put asunder.

—New Testament: Mark 10:6–9

Thou shalt not covet thy neighbor's wife.
—Old Testament: Exodus 20:17

They [the priests] shall not take a wife that is a whore, or profane; neither shall they take a woman put away from her husband.

—Old Testament: Leviticus 21:7

If any man's wife go aside, and commit a trespass against him, . . . Then shall the man bring his wife unto the priest.

—Old Testament: Numbers 5:12

The remainder of the chapter is devoted to the details of the wife's trial and punishment.

And what man is there that hath betrothed a wife, and hath not taken her? let him go and return unto his house, lest he die in the battle, and another man take her.

—Old Testament: Deuteronomy 20:7

If any man take a wife, and go in unto her, and hate her, . . . And say, I took this woman, and when I came to her, I found her not a maid: Then shall the father of the damsel, and her mother, take and bring forth the tokens of the damsel's virginity unto the elders of the city in the gate. . . . And the elders of that city shall take that man and chastise him; . . . and she shall be his wife; he may not put her away all his days. But if this thing be true, and the tokens of virginity be not found for the damsel: . . . the men of her city shall stone her with stones that she die.

—Old Testament: Deuteronomy 22:13–21

Thy wife shall be as a fruitful vine by the sides of thine house: thy children like olive plants round about thy table.

—Old Testament: Psalms 128:3

Live joyfully with the wife whom thou lovest all the days of the life of thy vanity, which he hath given thee under the sun: . . . for that is thy portion in this life, and in the labor which thou takest under the sun.
—Old Testament: Ecclesiastes 9:9

Whoso findeth a wife findeth a good thing, and obtaineth favor of the Lord.
—Old Testament: Proverbs 18:22

If a man put away his wife, and she go from him, and become another man's, shall he return unto her again? shall not that land be greatly polluted?
—Old Testament: Jeremiah 3:1

Hast thou a wife after thy mind? forsake her not: give not thyself over to a light woman.
—Old Testament Apocrypha: Ecclesiasticus 7:26

Sit not at all with another man's wife, . . . and spend not thy money with her at wine; lest thine heart incline unto her, and so through thy desire thou fall into destruction.
—Old Testament Apocrypha: Ecclesiasticus 9:9

Blessed is the man that hath a virtuous wife, for the number of his days shall be double. A virtuous woman rejoiceth her husband, and he shall fulfill the years of his life in peace. A good wife is a good portion.
—Old Testament Apocrypha: Ecclesiasticus 26:1–3

A silent and loving woman is a gift of the Lord; . . . A shamefaced and faithful woman is a double grace.
—Old Testament Apocrypha: Ecclesiasticus 26:14–15

As the sun when it ariseth in the high heaven; so is the beauty of a good wife in the ordering of her house.
—Old Testament Apocrypha: Ecclesiasticus 26:16

I have married a wife, and cannot come.
—New Testament: Luke 14:20

Let every man have his own wife.
—New Testament: I Corinthians 7:2

Art thou bound unto a wife? seek not to be loosed. Art thou loosed from a wife? seek not a wife.
—New Testament: I Corinthians 7:27

He that loveth his wife loveth himself.
—New Testament: Ephesians 5:28
(HBBQ)

WILDERNESS–

Your carcasses shall fall in this wilderness. . . . And your children shall wander in the wilderness forty years, . . . until your carcasses be wasted in the wilderness. . . . In this wilderness they shall be consumed.
—Old Testament: Numbers 14:29–35

See also New Testament: Hebrews 3:17.

That great and terrible wilderness.
—Old Testament: Deuteronomy 1:19; 8:15

He turneth the wilderness into a standing water, and dry ground into watersprings. And there he maketh the hungry to dwell, that they may prepare a city for habitation; And sow the fields, and plant vineyards, which may yield fruits of increase.
—Old Testament: Psalms 107:35–37

The Lord . . . led us through the wilderness, through a land of deserts and of pits, through a land of drought, and of the shadow of death.
—Old Testament: Jeremiah 2:6

What went ye out into the wilderness to see?
—New Testament: Matthew 11:7; Luke 7:24

He carried me away in the spirit into the wilderness.
—New Testament: Revelation 17:3
(HBBQ)

WILL–

He did according to his will.
—Old Testament: Daniel 8:4; 11:3, 16, 36

According to the good pleasure of his will.
—New Testament: Ephesians 1:5; Hebrews 2:4; I John 5:14

Good will toward men.
—New Testament: Luke 2:14

Some indeed preach . . . of good will.
—New Testament: Philippians 1:15

Teach me to do thy will.
—Old Testament: Psalms 143:10

Thy will be done.
—New Testament: Matthew 6:10; 26:42; Luke 11:2

Not my will, but thine, be done.
—New Testament: Luke 22:42

The will of my Father which is in heaven.
—New Testament: Matthew 7:21; 12:50; 18:14

Whosoever shall do the will of God, the same is my brother, and my sister, and mother.
—New Testament: Mark 3:35

"The will of God" is frequently repeated.
(HBBQ)

WIND–

God made a wind to pass over the earth.
—Old Testament: Genesis 8:1

The designation (HBBQ) indicates material taken from THE HOME BOOK OF BIBLE QUOTATIONS; (DB) signifies the DICTIONARY OF THE BIBLE; and (HBP) is THE HANDBOOK OF BIBLICAL PERSONALITIES.

He that . . . createth the wind, . . . the Lord, the God of hosts, is his name.
—Old Testament: Amos 4:13

The Lord brought an east wind upon the land.
—Old Testament: Exodus 10:13

Should a wise man . . . fill his belly with the east wind?
—Old Testament: Job 15:2

The east wind hath broken thee in the midst of the seas.
—Old Testament: Ezekiel 27:26

An east wind shall come, the wind of the Lord shall come up from the wilderness, and his spring shall become dry.
—Old Testament: Hosea 13:15

The north wind driveth away rain.
—Old Testament: Proverbs 25:23

There went forth a wind from the Lord.
—Old Testament: Numbers 11:31

There came a great wind from the wilderness, and smote the four corners of the house.
—Old Testament: Job 1:19

The Lord sent out a great wind into the sea.
—Old Testament: Jonah 1:4

He was seen upon the wings of the wind.
—Old Testament: II Samuel 22:11

The wind passeth over it, and it is gone; and the place thereof shall know it no more.
—Old Testament: Psalms 103:16

He causeth his wind to blow, and the waters flow.
—Old Testament: Psalms 147:18

He that troubleth his own house shall inherit the wind.
—Old Testament: Proverbs 11:29

With his mighty wind shall he shake his hand over the river, and shall smite it in the seven streams, and make men go over dryshod.
—Old Testament: Isaiah 11:15

I will scatter unto all winds them that are in the utmost corners.
—Old Testament: Jeremiah 49:32, 36

The four winds of the heaven strove upon the great sea.
—Old Testament: Daniel 7:2

"The four winds of heaven" is repeated in 8:8, and 11:4.

I saw four angels standing on the four corners of the earth, holding the four winds of the earth.
—New Testament: Revelation 7:1

Then he arose, and rebuked the wind.
—New Testament: Matthew 8:26;
Mark 4:39; Luke 8:24

The wind bloweth where it listeth, and thou hearest the sound thereof, but canst not tell whence it cometh, and whither it goeth.
—New Testament: John 3:8
(HBBQ)

WINE—

He drank of the wine, and was drunken.
—Old Testament: Genesis 9:21

Melchizedek . . . brought forth bread and wine.
—Old Testament: Genesis 14:18

God gave thee . . . plenty of corn and wine.
—Old Testament: Genesis 27:28, 37

"Corn and wine" is frequently used.

Do not drink wine nor strong drink.
—Old Testament: Leviticus 10:9;
Judges 13:4, 7, 14;
New Testament: Luke 1:15

"Wine and strong drink" was used habitually to indicate all the fermented beverages then in use.

Thou . . . shalt neither drink of the wine, nor gather the grapes.
—Old Testament: Deuteronomy 28:39

The heart of the king was merry with wine.
—Old Testament: Esther 1:10

Wine that maketh glad the heart of man.
—Old Testament: Psalms 104:15

Wine maketh merry.
—Old Testament: Ecclesiastes 10:19

Thou hast made us to drink the wine of astonishment.
—Old Testament: Psalms 60:3

The wine is red; it is full of mixture.
—Old Testament: Psalms 75:8

The "mixture" or "mingling" refers to the practice of adding aromatic herbs and spices to the wine in order to add to its strength and flavor. Isaiah (5:22) denounced it.

Thy wine [is become] mixed with water.
—Old Testament: Isaiah 1:22

That is, diluted, adulterated.

Look not thou upon the wine when it is red, when it giveth his color in the cup, when it moveth itself aright. At the last it biteth like a serpent, and stingeth like an adder.
—Old Testament: Proverbs 23:31–32

Be not among winebibbers.
—Old Testament: Proverbs 23:20

A man gluttonous, and a winebibber.
—New Testament: Matthew 11:19; Luke 7:34

Give . . , . wine unto those that be of heavy hearts. Let him drink, and forget his poverty, and remember his misery no more.
—Old Testament: Proverbs 31:6–7

I have drunk my wine with my milk.
—Old Testament: Song of Solomon 5:1

The new wine mourneth, the vine languisheth, all the merryhearted do sigh.
—Old Testament: Isaiah 24:7

It shall come to pass in that day, that the mountains shall drop down new wine.
—Old Testament: Joel 3:18; Amos 9:13

No man putteth a piece of new cloth unto an old garment. . . . Neither do men put new wine into old bottles: else the bottles break, and the wine runneth out, and the bottles perish: but they put new wine into new bottles, and both are preserved.
—New Testament: Matthew 9:16–17; Mark 2:21–22; Luke 5:36–37

I set before the sons of the house of the Rechabites pots full of wine, and cups, and I said unto them, Drink ye wine. But they said, We will drink no wine; for . . . our father commanded us, saying, Ye shall drink no wine, neither ye, nor your sons for ever.
—Old Testament: Jeremiah 35:5–6

'Gather ye wine, and summer fruits, and oil, and put them in your vessels.
—Old Testament: Jeremiah 40:10, 12

How exceeding strong is wine! it causeth all men to err that drink it: It maketh the mind of the king and of the fatherless child to be all one; of the bondman and of the freeman, of the poor man and of the rich: It turneth also every thought into jollity and mirth, so that a man remembereth neither sorrow nor debt: And it maketh every heart rich.
—Old Testament Apocrypha: I Esdras 3:18–21

Wine and women will make men of understanding to fall away.
—Old Testament Apocrypha: Ecclesiasticus 19:2

Shew not thy valiantness in wine: for wine hath destroyed many. . . . Wine is as good as life to a man, if it be drunk moderately: what life is then to a man

that is without wine? for it was made to make men glad. Wine measurably drunk and in season bringeth gladness of the heart, and cheerfulness of the mind: But wine drunken with excess maketh bitterness of the mind, with brawling and quarreling.
—Old Testament Apocrypha: Ecclesiasticus 31:25–29

It is good neither to eat flesh, nor to drink wine, nor any thing whereby thy brother stumbleth, or is offended, or is made weak.
—New Testament: Romans 14:21

Be not drunk with wine, wherein is excess; but be filled with the Spirit.
—New Testament: Ephesians 5:18

Drink no longer water, but use a little wine for thy stomach's sake and thine often infirmities.
—New Testament: I Timothy 5:23

She made all nations drink of the wine of the wrath of her fornication.
—New Testament: Revelation 14:8; 17:2; 18:3
(HBBQ)

The production of wine is prehistoric in the Near East. The invention of wine is attributed to Noah (Genesis 9:20 f.), who is here a culture hero; the account takes a somewhat mixed view, since Noah first experiences intoxication. Wine was the usual drink with meals and is very frequently mentioned in the Bible. Palestine itself was a wine producing country; some wines of other regions are mentioned as especially good (Lebanon, Hosea 14:8; Helbon, Ezekiel 27:18). Greek levels of occupation in Palestine contain many stamped Rhodian jar handles; the wine of Rhodes was prized in the ancient world. Wine is a gift and a blessing of Yahweh, which He withdraws in punishment. The wine press usually stood in the vineyard; the excavations at Gibeon, which show that this town was an important center of wine manufacture, have uncovered several such installations, which appear at other sites also. The press consisted of two troughs cut in a rock at different levels with a drain leading from the upper level to the lower level. The first press was done by treading with the feet (Nehemiah 13:15); this was a festive occupation carried on with shouts and to the accompaniment of music. The grapes were then pressed by means of a beam weighted with a stone or by the use of poles which served as levers for weights. The treading of the grapes is a figure for the punishing wrath of Yahweh. The juice was

The designation (HBBQ) indicates material taken from THE HOME BOOK OF BIBLE QUOTATIONS; (DB) signifies the DICTIONARY OF THE BIBLE; and (HBP) is THE HANDBOOK OF BIBLICAL PERSONALITIES.

stored in vats or in skin vessels for fermentation; new skins were necessary for this process. No method of storing unfermented juice was known. The excavations of Gibeon disclosed over 40 large vats cut in the rock with a capacity of several thousand gallons each. Some of these were plastered and could store wine in such large quantities; most were unplastered and must have held the wine in jars. The temperature of the vats when covered was a constant 65° F at all seasons. Wine was not only taken with meals but was also carried as part of the provision of the traveler and is noted as part of the provisions of garrison troops. Wine was cut with water in the Greek period, and Isaiah 1:22 indicates that it was done also in the earlier periods, although it is not praised in this passage. The Israelites also very probably flavored their wine with spices as other peoples did. . . . Intemperance was common enough, and the Bible contains a number of unfavorable references to excessive drinking. . . .

The attitude of Jesus toward wine, like that of the entire Bible, is neutral, praising its use and finding fault in its intemperate use. Certainly the production of wine at Cana (John 2:1–11) scarcely supports any belief that Jesus or the primitive Church regarded the use of wine as sinful in itself.

The religious use of wine in the Old Testament is not important. It accompanies sacrifices as a libation. The abstinence from wine practiced by the Nazirites and the Rechabites was due to the peculiar vow and the peculiar traditions respectively.

(DB)

WINGS–

They shall mount up with wings as eagles.
—Old Testament: Isaiah 40:31

The Lord God of Israel, under whose wings thou art come to trust.
—Old Testament: Ruth 2:12

Hide me under the shadow of thy wings.
—Old Testament: Psalms 17:8

In the shadow of thy wings will I make my refuge.
—Old Testament: Psalms 57:1

Gavest thou the goodly wings unto the peacocks? or wings and feathers unto the ostrich?
—Old Testament: Job 39:13

The only use of "ostrich." "Ostriches" occurs in Lamentations 4:3, "Like the ostriches in the wilderness."

Oh that I had wings like a dove! for then would I fly away, and be at rest.
—Old Testament: Psalms 55:6

The wings of the morning.
—Old Testament: Psalms 139:9

Upon the wings of the wind.
—Old Testament: II Samuel 22:11;
Psalms 18:10; 104:3

The stretching out of his wings shall fill the breadth of thy land.
—Old Testament: Isaiah 8:8
(HBBQ)

WINTER–

And the Lord said in his heart, . . . While the earth remaineth . . . cold and heat, and summer and winter, and day and night shall not cease.
—Old Testament: Genesis 8:21–22

Thou hast made summer and winter.
—Old Testament: Psalms 74:17

For, lo, the winter is past, the rain is over and gone. The flowers appear on the earth; the time of the singing of birds is come, and the voice of the turtle is heard in our land; The fig tree putteth forth her green figs, and the vines with the tender grape give a good smell.
—Old Testament: Song of Solomon 2:11–13
(HBBQ)

WISDOM–

In the hearts of all that are wise hearted I have put wisdom.
—Old Testament: Exodus 31:6

All the women that were wise hearted did spin with their hands. . . . And all the women whose heart stirred them up in wisdom spun goats' hair.
—Old Testament: Exodus 35:25

The wise in heart shall be called prudent.
—Old Testament: Proverbs 16:21

God gave Solomon wisdom and understanding.
—Old Testament: I Kings 4:29

The Lord gave thee wisdom and understanding.
—Old Testament: I Chronicles 22:12

He that handleth a matter wisely shall find good.
—Old Testament: Proverbs 16:20

Take you wise men and understanding, . . . and I will make them rulers over you.
—Old Testament: Deuteronomy 1:13

My lord is wise, according to the wisdom of an angel of God, to know all things that are in the earth.
—Old Testament: II Samuel 14:20

Do therefore according to thy wisdom.
—Old Testament: I Kings 2:6

I cannot find one wise man among you.
—Old Testament: Job 17:10

O that God . . . would shew thee the secrets of wisdom.
—Old Testament: Job 11:5–6

With the ancient is wisdom. . . . With him is wisdom and strength.
—Old Testament: Job 12:12–13

Where shall wisdom be found? and where is the place of understanding? Man knoweth not the price thereof; neither is it found in the land of the living. The depth saith, It is not in me: and the sea saith, It is not with me.
It cannot be gotten for gold, neither shall silver be weighed for the price thereof. It cannot be valued with the gold of Ophir, with the precious onyx, or the sapphire. . . . No mention shall be made of coral, or of pearls: for the price of wisdom is above rubies.
—Old Testament: Job 28:12–18

Whence then cometh wisdom? and where is the place of understanding? . . . God understandeth the way thereof, and he knoweth the place thereof. . . . And unto man he said, Behold, the fear of the Lord, that is wisdom; and to depart from evil is understanding.
—Old Testament: Job 28:20–28

Hold thy peace, and I shall teach thee wisdom.
—Old Testament: Job 33:33

So teach us to number our days, that we may apply our hearts unto wisdom.
—Old Testament: Psalms 90:12

Rebuke a wise man, and he will love thee. Give instruction to a wise man, and he will be yet wiser.
—Old Testament: Proverbs 9:8–9

Wisdom crieth without; she uttereth her voice in the streets, saying, . . . Behold, I will pour out my spirit unto you.
—Old Testament: Proverbs 1:20–23

Happy is the man that findeth wisdom. . . . She is more precious than rubies. . . . Length of days is in her right hand; and in her left hand riches and honor. Her ways are ways of pleasantness, and all her paths are peace. She is a tree of life to them that lay hold upon her: and happy is every one that retaineth her.
—Old Testament: Proverbs 3:13–18

Get wisdom, get understanding. . . . Forsake her not, and she shall preserve thee: love her, and she shall keep thee. Wisdom is the principal thing; therefore get wisdom: . . . Exalt her, and she shall promote thee: she shall bring thee to honor, when thou dost embrace her. She shall give to thine head an ornament of grace: a crown of glory shall she deliver to thee.
—Old Testament: Proverbs 4:5–9

Be not wise in thine own eyes.
—Old Testament: Proverbs 3:7

Wise in his own conceit.
—Old Testament: Proverbs 26:5, 12, 16; 28:11

Wise in your own conceits.
—New Testament: Romans 11:25; 12:16

A man shall be commended according to his wisdom.
—Old Testament: Proverbs 12:8

Wisdom resteth in the heart of him that hath understanding.
—Old Testament: Proverbs 14:33

How much better is it to get wisdom than gold!
—Old Testament: Proverbs 16:16

He that hearkeneth unto counsel is wise.
—Old Testament: Proverbs 12:15

He that getteth wisdom loveth his own soul.
—Old Testament: Proverbs 19:8

Wise men turn away wrath.
—Old Testament: Proverbs 29:8

God giveth to a man that is good in his sight wisdom, and knowledge, and joy.
—Old Testament: Ecclesiastes 2:26

A man's wisdom maketh his face to shine.
—Old Testament: Ecclesiastes 8:1

The wise, and their works, are in the hand of God.
—Old Testament: Ecclesiastes 9:1

Wisdom and knowledge shall be the stability of thy times, and strength of salvation.
—Old Testament: Isaiah 33:6

Let not the wise man glory in his wisdom.
—Old Testament: Jeremiah 9:23

With thy wisdom and with thine understanding thou hast gotten thee riches.
—Old Testament: Ezekiel 28:4, 5

They that be wise shall shine as the brightness of the firmament.
—Old Testament: Daniel 12:3

The designation (HBBQ) indicates material taken from THE HOME BOOK OF BIBLE QUOTATIONS; (DB) signifies the DICTIONARY OF THE BIBLE; and (HBP) is THE HANDBOOK OF BIBLICAL PERSONALITIES.

Into a malicious soul wisdom shall not enter; nor dwell in the body that is subject unto sin. . . . For wisdom is a loving spirit; and will not acquit a blasphemer of his words.
—Old Testament Apocryphia: Wisdom of Solomon 1:4, 6

Wisdom is glorious, and never fadeth away: yea, she is easily seen of them that love her, and found of such as seek her. . . . For she goeth about seeking such as are worthy of her.
—Old Testament Apocrypha: Wisdom of Solomon 6:12–16

The desire of wisdom bringeth to a kingdom. If your delight be then in thrones and sceptres, O ye kings of the people, honor wisdom, that ye may reign for evermore. . . . The multitude of the wise is the welfare of the world.
—Old Testament Apocrypha: Wisdom of Solomon 6:20–24

Wisdom . . . I preferred before sceptres and thrones, and esteemed riches nothing in comparison of her. Neither compared I unto her any precious stone, because all gold in respect of her is as a little sand, and silver shall be counted as clay before her. I loved her above health and beauty, and chose to have her instead of light: for the light that cometh from her never goeth out. All good things together came to me with her, and innumerable riches in her hands. And I rejoiced in them all, because wisdom goeth before them.
—Old Testament Apocrypha: Wisdom of Solomon 7:7–12

Wisdom opened the mouth of the dumb, and made the tongues of them that cannot speak eloquent.
—Old Testament Apocrypha: Wisdom of Solomon 10:21

[He] did not only gather the grave and short sentences of wise men, that had been before him, but himself also uttered some of his own full of much understanding and wisdom. . . . Sirach compiled it all orderly into one volume, and called it Wisdom. . . . It containeth therefore wise sayings, dark sentences, and parables, and certain particular ancient godly stories of men that pleased God.
—Old Testament Apocrypha: Ecclesiasticus: Prologue

Said to have been written by Athanasius. The reference is to Jesus, the grandfather of Jesus, the son of Sirach, who lived about 190 B.C., and compiled Ecclesiasticus, or "Book of the Church," a name given it in the African church, because of its use there as a book of instruction.

The word of God most high is the fountain of wisdom; and her ways are everlasting commandments.
—Old Testament Apocrypha: Ecclesiasticus 1:5

Wisdom exalteth her children, and layeth hold of them that seek her. He that loveth her loveth life; . . . He that holdeth her fast shall inherit glory; and wheresoever she entereth, the Lord will bless. . . . Them that love her the Lord doth love.
—Old Testament Apocrypha: Ecclesiasticus 4:11–14

Wisdom that is hid, and treasure that is hoarded up, what profit is in them both? Better is he that hideth his folly than a man that hideth his wisdom.
—Old Testament Apocrypha: Ecclesiasticus 20:30–31; 41:14–15

Wisdom shall praise herself, and shall glory in the midst of her people. . . . Come unto me, all ye that be desirous of me, and fill yourselves with my fruits. For my memorial is sweeter than honey, and mine inheritance than the honeycomb.
—Old Testament Apocrypha: Ecclesiasticus 24:1, 19–20

A wise man shall be filled with blessing; and all they that see him shall count him happy. . . . A wise man shall inherit glory among his people, and his name shall be perpetual.
—Old Testament: Ecclesiasticus 37:24, 26

Learn where is wisdom, where is strength, where is understanding; that thou mayest know also where is length of days.
—Old Testament Apocrypha: Baruch 3:14

There came wise men from the east.
—New Testament: Matthew 2:1

Be ye therefore wise as serpents.
—New Testament: Matthew 10:16

Not many wise men after the flesh . . . are called.
—New Testament: I Corinthians 1:26

Is it so, that there is not a wise man among you?
—New Testament: I Corinthians 6:5

Who is a wise man and endued with knowledge among you? let him shew out of a good conversation his works with meekness of wisdom. But if ye have bitter envying and strife in your hearts, glory not, and lie not against the truth. This wisdom descendeth not from above, but is earthly, sensual, devilish.
—New Testament: James 3:13–15

It is written, I will destroy the wisdom of the wise. . . . Where is the wise? where is the scribe? where is the disputer of this world? hath not God made foolish the wisdom of this world?
—New Testament: I Corinthians 1:19–20

The only use of "disputer." The reference is to Isaiah 29:14, "The wisdom of their wise men shall perish."

We speak not in the words which man's wisdom teacheth, but which the Holy Ghost teacheth; comparing spiritual things with spiritual.
—New Testament: I Corinthians 2:13

Walk in wisdom toward them that are without.
—New Testament: Colossians 4:5

If any of you lack wisdom, let him ask of God, . . . and it shall be given him. But let him ask in faith, nothing wavering. For he that wavereth is like a wave of the sea driven with the wind and tossed.

—New Testament: James 1:5–6

Where envying and strife is, there is confusion and every evil work. But wisdom that is from above is first pure, then peaceable, gentle, and easy to be intreated, full of mercy and good fruits, without partiality, and without hypocrisy.

—New Testament: James 3:16–17

"Partiality" is used only once again, in I Timothy 5:21, "Doing nothing by partiality."

(HBBQ)

WITCH OF ENDOR, THE–

I Samuel 28:7 f.

Although the text of the story calls the woman a "medium" or "the woman," she is popularly known as the "Witch of Endor."

Saul had attempted to put an end to the practice of magic and witchcraft among the tribes. He killed some who had "familiar spirits," and announced that sorcery would be punishable by death henceforth. Yet he was not convinced that divination by sorcerers and "mediums" should be wholly stamped out, and the practice went underground.

After the death of Samuel, Saul's troubles with the Philistines and his anxiety over the rising prominence of David reduced him to a state of apathy. He "enquired of the Lord and the Lord answered him not, neither by dreams, nor by Urim, nor by prophets." Desperate, he disguised himself and at night sought out "a woman that hath a familiar spirit" to ask that she "bring up" the shade of Samuel, from whom he hoped to receive counsel and consolation.

The woman at Endor did call up Samuel's ghost, but Saul received no comfort, for Samuel confirmed the fact that the Lord had departed from Saul and predicted further that on the morrow "shalt thou and thy sons be with me."

Saul was "sore troubled" at the prediction and refused further ministrations from the woman until his servants insisted that he eat the meal she had prepared for them. She was afraid to have Saul in her house and anxious that from the meal he should receive strength to be on his way before daylight; for, having recognized him, she knew that her life was "in his hands."

(HBP)*

WITNESS–

Let it be for a witness between me and thee.

—Old Testament: Genesis 31:44

Let us . . . build us an altar: . . . that it may be a witness between us and you.

—Old Testament: Joshua 22:26–27, 28

Put thine hand with the wicked to be an unrighteous witness.

—Old Testament: Exodus 23:1

One witness shall not testify against any person to cause him to die.

—Old Testament: Numbers 35:30

One witness shall not rise up against a man for any iniquity, or for any sin: . . . at the mouth of two witnesses, or at the mouth of three witnesses, shall the matter be established.

—Old Testament: Deuteronomy 19:15

Ye are witnesses against yourselves.

—Old Testament: Joshua 24:22

My witness is in heaven, and my record is on high.

—Old Testament: Job 16:19

Be not a witness against thy neighbor without cause.

—Old Testament: Proverbs 24:28

I know, and am a witness, saith the Lord.

—Old Testament: Jeremiah 29:23

Ye be witnesses unto yourselves.

—New Testament: Matthew 23:31

Ye shall be witnesses unto me . . . unto the uttermost part of the earth.

—New Testament: Acts 1:8

We are his witnesses of these things. . . . Witnesses of all things which he did both in the land of the Jews, and in Jerusalem.

—New Testament: Acts 5:32; 10:39

Thou shalt be his witness unto all men of what thou hast seen and heard.

—New Testament: Acts 22:15

Thou shalt not bear false witness against thy neighbor.

—Old Testament: Exodus 20:16;
Deuteronomy 5:20; New Testament:
Matthew 19:18; Romans 13:9

If a false witness rise up against any man to testify against him that which is wrong; . . . Then shall ye do unto him, as he had thought to have done unto his brother.

—Old Testament: Deuteronomy 19:16–19

The designation (HBBQ) indicates material taken from THE HOME BOOK OF BIBLE QUOTATIONS; (DB) signifies the DICTIONARY OF THE BIBLE; and (HBP) is THE HANDBOOK OF BIBLICAL PERSONALITIES.

A faithful witness will not lie: but a false witness will utter lies.
—Old Testament: Proverbs 14:5

Many bare false witness against him, but their witness agreed not together.
—New Testament: Mark 14:56
(HBBQ)

WOMAN–

And the Lord caused a deep sleep to fall upon Adam and he slept: and he took one of his ribs, and closed up the flesh instead thereof; And the rib which the Lord God had taken from man, made he a woman, and brought her unto the man. And Adam said, This is now bone of my bones, and flesh of my flesh: she shall be called Woman, because she was taken out of Man.
—Old Testament: Genesis 2:21–23

The Hebrew word is ishshah.

And the man said, the woman whom thou gavest to be with me, she gave me of the tree, and I did eat.
—Old Testament: Genesis 3:12

If a woman have an issue, and her issue in her flesh be blood, she shall be put apart seven days: and whosoever toucheth her shall be unclean until the even. . . . And if any man lie with her at all, and her flowers be upon him, he shall be unclean seven days.
—Old Testament: Leviticus 15:19–24

See also 15:33. The only uses of "flowers" in this sense. The Hebrew word is niddah, *impurity.*

If a man shall lie with a woman having her sickness, . . . both of them shall be cut off from among their people.
—Old Testament: Leviticus 20:18

The woman also with whom man shall lie with seed of copulation, they shall both bathe themselves in water, and be unclean until the even.
—Old Testament: Leviticus 15:18

The phrase "seed of copulation" is repeated in 16 and 17, and occurs nowhere else.

The woman shall not wear that which pertaineth unto a man.
—Old Testament: Deuteronomy 22:5

I will . . . that women adorn themselves in modest apparel, with shamefacedness and sobriety; not with broidered hair, or gold, or pearls, or costly array; But (which becometh women professing godliness) with good works.
—New Testament: I Timothy 2:9–10

The only use of "shamefacedness."

The tender and delicate woman among you, which would not adventure to set the sole of her foot upon the ground for delicateness and tenderness, her eye shall be evil toward the husband of her bosom.
—Old Testament: Deuteronomy 28:56

A virtuous woman is a crown to her husband: but she that maketh ashamed is as rottenness in his bones.
—Old Testament: Proverbs 12:4

How can he be clean that is born of a woman?
—Old Testament: Job 25:4

The lips of a strange woman drop as an honeycomb, and her mouth is smoother than oil. But her end is bitter as wormwood, sharp as a two-edged sword. Her feet go down to death; her steps take hold on hell. . . . Remove thy way far from her, and come not nigh the door of her house: Lest thou give thine honor unto others, and thy years unto the cruel: Lest strangers be filled with thy wealth; and thy labors be in the house of a stranger; And thou mourn at the last, when thy flesh and thy body are consumed.
—Old Testament: Proverbs 5:3–11

My son, keep thy father's commandment, . . . For the commandment is a lamp, . . . To keep thee from the evil woman, from the flattery of the tongue of a strange woman. Lust not after her beauty in thine heart; neither let her take thee with her eyelids. For by means of a whorish woman a man is brought to a piece of bread.
—Old Testament: Proverbs 6:20–26

A foolish woman is clamorous: she is simple, and knoweth nothing. For she sitteth at the door of her house, . . . To call passengers who go right on their ways: Whoso is simple, let him turn in hither: And as for him that wanteth understanding, she saith to him, Stolen waters are sweet, and bread eaten in secret is pleasant. But he knoweth not that the dead are there; and that her guests are in the depths of hell.
—Old Testament: Proverbs 9:13–18

In that day seven women shall take hold of one man, saying, We will eat our own bread, and wear our own apparel: only let us be called by thy name, to take away our reproach.
—Old Testament: Isaiah 4:1

Tremble, ye women that are at ease; be troubled, ye careless ones: strip you, and make you bare, and gird sackcloth upon your loins.
—Old Testament: Isaiah 32:11

The Lord hath created a new thing in the earth, A woman shall compass a man.
—Old Testament: Jeremiah 31:22

Give not thy soul unto a woman to set her foot upon thy substance.
—Old Testament Apocrypha: Ecclesiasticus 9:2

Stumble not at the beauty of a woman, and desire her not for pleasure.
—Old Testament Apocrypha: Ecclesiasticus 25:21

A woman when she is in travail hath sorrow, because her hour is come: but as soon as she is delivered of the child, she remembereth no more the anguish, for joy that a man is born into the world.
—New Testament: John 16:21

And there appeared a great wonder in heaven; a woman clothed with the sun, and the moon under her feet, and upon her head a crown of twelve stars: And she being with child cried, travailing in birth, and pained to be delivered.

—New Testament: Revelation 12:1

Let your women keep silence in the churches: for it is not permitted unto them to speak; . . . And if they will learn any thing, let them ask their husbands at home: for it is a shame for women to speak in the church.

—New Testament: I Corinthians 14:34–35

I will therefore that the younger women marry, bear children, guide the house, give none occasion to the adversary to speak reproachfully.

—New Testament: I Timothy 5:14

The aged women . . . may teach the younger women to be sober, to love their husbands, to love their children, To be discreet, chaste, keepers at home, good, obedient to their own husbands.

—New Testament: Titus 2:4–5
(HBBQ)

1. *In the Near East, Greece, and Rome.*

In the ancient Near East woman generally had no rights as a free person; she was always subject to a man, either her father or husband. By chance a section of the Middle Assyrian laws which have survived deals almost entirely with women. These laws may not be altogether representative of Mesopotamia; in many respects their casual treatment of woman, such as retaliation of damages on the innocent wife or daughter of the offender, is savage. But even these laws admit a kind of common law marriage and suppose that a widow may have property of her own; if a widow marries and moves into her husband's house, he acquires all her property; but if the husband moves into her house, she acquires all his property. Legal practice in Mesopotamia, at least in some periods and in some places, permitted woman to act as a legal agent; women appear as owners, buyers, sellers, defendants, and plaintiffs in contracts.

The legal inferiority of woman is paradoxically opposed to the conception of the fertility goddess who is wife and mother. The goddess represents woman as the source of life; but she also represents woman as the instrument of sexual pleasure, and in the grosser conceptions of the cult this is her highest function. It seems that the overemphasis upon the sexual function of woman in-volved a loss of dignity as a member of society and as a full partner in matrimony. It is apparent from the laws of Mesopotamia that a high degree of freedom and possibly a position of greater esteem and dignity belonged to women of the temple personnel, whether priestesses or cultic prostitutes.

While it is difficult to generalize about the position of women in Greece, it is clear that at Athens the wife had a social position almost as low as the woman of the east: her life was strictly confined to the home and her one responsibility was the bearing and rearing of legitimate children. It was accepted that the womanly graces and the cultivation of wit and intelligence were permitted only to the professional companions (*hetaera*), who were more than mere prostitutes; they furnished entertaining conversation and diversions. As in the Near East, marital fidelity was not imposed upon the husband. Greek marriage, however, was monogamous. Both in Greece and in the Near East there are numerous allusions to the popular belief that woman is by instinct a nymphomaniac; it is assumed that no woman can be trusted to remain faithful unless she is closely watched.

Roman law and custom imposed a severe power of the father over both sons and daughters (*patria potestas*); but the position of the wife and mother of a family was higher both in legal rights and in dignity than in Greece or the east. Indeed, in the period of the later Republic and the early empire (the period of the New Testament) many contemporary writers regarded the freedom of women to associate freely with men and to share their social activities and public entertainments, such as the theater and the games, as a social deterioration. The freedom of women in Rome imposed no restraint upon sexual license either for men or for women. The excavations of Pompeii have disclosed that this ancient resort town was a vast brothel.

2. *In the Old Testament.* . . . While the legal position of Hebrew women was perhaps inferior to the position of women in Mesopotamia, their social position and dignity seem to have been superior. The mother is expressly included in the precepts of honor and obedience which sons must pay to parents. Women took part in festive celebrations; indeed, their song and dancing was one of the

The designation (HBBQ) indicates material taken from THE HOME BOOK OF BIBLE QUOTATIONS; (DB) signifies the DICTIONARY OF THE BIBLE; and (HBP) is THE HANDBOOK OF BIBLICAL PERSONALITIES.

principal elements of the celebration. . . . The women of the Bible whose stories are related because of their intelligence or devotion form an interesting group: Rahab, Michal, Abigail, Rizpah, the woman of Shunem; the pictures of the wives of patriarchs—Sarah, Hagar, Rebekah, Rachel, Leah —and of Jezebel, Delilah, and Athaliah are more mixed, but one can hardly say that women of this type represent a depressed class. Deborah is a Hebrew heroine, and the women of Ruth are depicted with all the qualities of womanhood. In later literature Judith and Esther are heroines. . . .

The most significant Old Testament passage which deals with the position of woman is Genesis 2–3. In Genesis 2 woman is represented as a helper "like man," of his species, "bone of his bone and flesh of his flesh," for whom man leaves his parents and lives with his wife. Equality seems to be implied in the narrative; and the implication is made clear in Genesis 3:16, where the existing inferiority of woman, her subjection to the man and her dependence upon him for sexual fulfillment which is the root of her subjection, is attributed to a curse. The inferiority of woman is thus presented as a deterioration from the primitive and unspoiled condition of man.

The work of women was long and hard; theirs were the milling, the baking, the procuring of fuel and water, spinning, weaving, sewing, the care of the house (in nomadic life the care and pitching and striking of the tent as well as its manufacture), the care of children. It is altogether probable that, like women in the modern Near East, they also shared in the tilling of the soil: plowing and sowing, reaping, threshing, although these are properly the responsibilities of men. The responsibilities of the Hebrew woman, however, were partly compensated by the freedom of movement which she enjoyed within the community, whether she were a wife or an unmarried daughter. . . .

The wisdom literature of the Old Testament exhibits a strain which can only be called misogyny. . . . The misogyny of the sages is an indirect testimonial that woman was not the depressed and helpless thing which one might deduce from studying the law alone. Misogyny reaches an even higher pitch in the rabbinical literature; the wise man thanks God that he has not made him a Gentile or a slave or a woman.

3. *In the New Testament.* The New Testament attitude toward women is hardly revolutionary in the proper sense; yet it proposes principles which are in opposition both to the social and legal depression of women of the east and the excessive emancipation of women in Rome.

The dealings of Jesus with women are revealing. He has an awareness of the daily life and tasks of women and an interest in them which is shown in the parables. . . . He performs miracles at the request of women just as He performs them for men. . . . His needs were served by a group of devoted women, many of whom witnessed His death and resurrection. His relations with Martha and Mary were those of close and familiar friendship. He spoke without embarrassment to a strange woman at the well of Jacob, which the disciples apparently thought a departure from good form (John 4:7 f., 27). These episodes reveal in Jesus a total absence of the misogyny and the assumption of the inferiority of woman which prevailed in the Jewish world of His time. His teaching in this respect is not revolutionary, but His conduct is. . . .

The theoretical position of woman is not often mentioned outside of the discussion of marriage, but the few texts are important. I Timothy 2:15, which affirms that women will be saved through motherhood, does not go beyond the Old Testament conception of woman's fulfillment. I Peter 3:7 affirms that woman is a full partner with man of the Christian life, but urges that she be cherished because she is the weaker sex; the weakness meant here is probably not merely physical. In Paul a certain tension appears. Woman is and ought to be subject to man, and Paul adduces theological arguments to show that the subjection should be maintained. On the other hand, he affirms the mutual interdependence of the two sexes (I Corinthians 11:11–12) and affirms that in Christ there is no difference between male and female, the clearest statement of the dignity of woman in the New Testament. The apparent antinomy probably arises because Paul, conditioned by the customs of the society in which he lived, saw in the emancipation of woman in the Roman world a breakdown of genuine morality. Rather than surrender to the general relaxed morals Christians should maintain what to Paul was the traditional and solid basis of Jewish family life, even though he knew that the subjection of women was the result of a curse. With the removal of the curse of sin the subjection should be removed, but not by a sudden upheavel of society. The principle is established, and as men and women grow in the life of regeneration woman also will recover the position which is rightly hers by nature and lost by sin.

(DB)

WOMB–

When the Lord saw, . . . he opened her womb.
—Old Testament: Genesis 29:31; 30:22

Every male that openeth the womb shall be called holy.
—New Testament: Luke 2:23

Naked came I out of my mother's womb.
—Old Testament: Job 1:21

Wherefore then hast thou brought me forth out of the womb? Oh that I had given up the ghost, and no eye had seen me! I should have been as though I had not been; I should have been carried from the womb to the grave.
—Old Testament: Job 10:18–19

Thou art he that took me out of the womb: . . . I was cast upon thee from the womb.
—Old Testament: Psalms 22:9–10

The babe leaped in her womb.
—New Testament: Luke 1:41, 44

Blessed are the barren, and the wombs that never bare.
—New Testament: Luke 23:29
(HBBQ)

WONDER–

There be three things which are too wonderful for me, yea, four which I know not: The way of an eagle in the air; the way of a serpent upon a rock; the way of a ship in the midst of the sea; and the way of a man with a maid.
—Old Testament: Proverbs 30:18–19

There appeared a great wonder in heaven.
—New Testament: Revelation 12:1, 3

Behold ye, . . . regard, and wonder marvelously.
—Old Testament: Habakkuk 1:5

I will shew wonders in heaven above, and signs in the earth beneath.
—New Testament: Acts 2:19

Many wonders and signs were done by the apostles.
—New Testament: Acts 2:43
(HBBQ)

WORD–

The word of the Lord came unto Abram in a vision. . . . Behold, the word of the Lord came unto him.
—Old Testament: Genesis 15:1, 4

The word of our God shall stand for ever.
—Old Testament: Isaiah 40:8

The word of the Lord endureth for ever.
—New Testament: I Peter 1:25

Blessed are they that hear the word of God and keep it.
—New Testament: Luke 11:28

The word of God is quick and powerful, and sharper than any two-edged sword.
—New Testament: Hebrews 4:12

"The word of the Lord" or "The word of God" is repeated many times.

They . . . brought back word.
—Old Testament: Numbers 13:26; Deuteronomy 1:25; Joshua 22:32

The Lord answered . . . with good words and comfortable words.
—Old Testament: Zechariah 1:13

"Comfortable" is used only once again, in II Samuel 14:17, "The word of my lord the king shall now be comfortable."

Let no man deceive you with vain words.
—New Testament: Ephesians 5:6

The word which I shall say unto thee, that shalt thou do.
—Old Testament: Numbers 22:20

The word that God putteth in my mouth, that shall I speak.
—Old Testament: Numbers 22:38

A man . . . shall not break his word.
—Old Testament: Numbers 30:2

Therefore shall ye lay up these my words in your heart and in your soul, and bind them for a sign upon your hand, that they may be as frontlets between your eyes.
—Old Testament: Deuteronomy 11:18

The last phrase is a repetition of Deuteronomy 6:8. "Frontlets" is used a third time in Exodus 13:16, "For frontlets between thine eyes."

Hear, O earth, the words of my mouth.
—Old Testament: Deuteronomy 32:1

How long shall the words of thy mouth be like a strong wind?
—Old Testament: Job 8:2

The designation (HBBQ) indicates material taken from THE HOME BOOK OF BIBLE QUOTATIONS; (DB) signifies the DICTIONARY OF THE BIBLE; and (HBP) is THE HANDBOOK OF BIBLICAL PERSONALITIES.

How long will ye vex my soul, and break me in pieces with words?
　　　　　　　　—Old Testament: Job 19:2

Oh that my words were now written! oh that they were printed in a book! That they were graven with an iron pen and lead in the rock for ever!
　　　　　　　　—Old Testament: Job 19:23–24

Hear my words, O ye wise men; and give ear unto me, ye that have knowledge.
　　　　　　　　—Old Testament: Job 34:2

Give ear to my words.
　　　　　　　　—Old Testament: Psalms 5:1; 54:2

Let the words of my mouth . . . be acceptable in thy sight.
　　　　　　　　—Old Testament: Psalms 19:14

The Lord gave the word: great was the company of those that published it.
　　　　　　　　—Old Testament: Psalms 68:11

Thy word have I hid in mine heart, that I might not sin against thee.
　　　　　　　　—Old Testament: Psalms 119:11

How sweet are thy words unto my taste! yea, sweeter than honey to my mouth!
　　　　　　　　—Old Testament: Psalms 119:103

Thy word is a lamp unto my feet, and a light unto my path.
　　　　　　　　—Old Testament: Psalms 119:105

Hear me now therefore, O ye children, and depart not from the words of my mouth.
　　　　　　　　—Old Testament: Proverbs 5:7

In the multitude of words there wanteth not sin.
　　　　　　　　—Old Testament: Proverbs 10:19

Let thy words be few.
　　　　　　　　—Old Testament: Ecclesiastes 5:2

A word spoken in due season, how good is it!
　　　　　　　　—Old Testament: Proverbs 15:23

The words of a man's mouth are as deep waters, and the wellspring of wisdom as a flowing brook.
　　　　　　　　—Old Testament: Proverbs 18:4

"Wellspring" is used once again in Proverbs 16:22, "Understanding is a wellspring of life."

As the rain cometh down, and the snow from heaven, and returneth not thither, . . . So shall my word be that goeth forth out of my mouth: it shall not return unto me void, but it shall accomplish that which I please.
　　　　　　　　—Old Testament: Isaiah 55:10–11

Is not my word like as a fire? saith the Lord; and like a hammer that breaketh the rock in pieces?
　　　　　　　　—Old Testament: Jeremiah 23:29

Speak the word only, and my servant shall be healed.
　　　　　　　　—New Testament: Matthew 8:8; Luke 7:7

Every idle word that men shall speak, they shall give account thereof in the day of judgment. For by thy words thou shalt be justified, and by thy words thou shalt be condemned.
　　　　　　　　—New Testament: Matthew 12:36–37

Heaven and earth shall pass away, but my words shall not pass away.
　　　　　　　　—New Testament: Matthew 24:35;
　　　　　　　　Mark 13:31; Luke 21:33

They were all amazed, and spake among themselves, saying, What a word is this! for with authority and power he commandeth the unclean spirits, and they come out.
　　　　　　　　—New Testament: Luke 4:36

In the beginning was the Word, and the Word was with God, and the Word was God. . . . In him was life; and the life was the light of men. And the light shineth in darkness; and the darkness comprehend it not.
　　　　　　　　—New Testament: John 1:1–5

If a man love me, he will keep my words.
　　　　　　　　—New Testament: John 14:23

The word which ye hear is not mine, but the Father's which sent me.
　　　　　　　　—New Testament: John 14:24

Thy word is truth.
　　　　　　　　—New Testament: John 17:17

As newborn babes, desire the sincere milk of the word, that ye may grow thereby.
　　　　　　　　—New Testament: I Peter 2:2

My son, blemish not thy good deeds, neither use uncomfortable words when thou givest any thing. Shall not the dew assuage the heat? so is a word better than a gift.
　　　　　　　　—Old Testament Apocrypha: Ecclesiasticus 18:15–16

They say, and do not.
　　　　　　　　—New Testament: Matthew 23:3

Mighty in deed and word.
　　　　　　　　—New Testament: Luke 24:19

Whatsoever ye do in word or deed, do all in the name of the Lord Jesus.
　　　　　　　　—New Testament: Colossians 3:17

Be ye doers of the word, and not hearers only, . . . For if any be a hearer of the word, and not a doer, he is like unto a man beholding his natural face in a glass: For he beholdeth himself, and goeth his way, and straightway forgetteth what manner of man he was.
　　　　　　　　—New Testament: James 1:22–24
　　　　　　　　(HBBQ)

WORK, WORKS–

On the seventh day God ended his work, . . . and . . . rested from all his work.
—Old Testament: Genesis 2:2–3

Six days shalt thou labor, and do all thy work.
—Old Testament: Exodus 20:9. See also Exodus 31:14–15; 23:12; 35:2; Leviticus 23:3; Deuteronomy 4:13–14.

How great are thy works!
—Old Testament: Psalms 92:5

[Do this] that the Lord thy God may bless thee in all the work of thine hand which thou doest.
—Old Testament: Deuteronomy 14:29

Is it good unto thee . . . that thou shouldest despise the work of thine hands?
—Old Testament: Job 10:3

"The work of thine hands" is repeated in Job 14:15; 34:19; Psalms 8:6; 28:4; 90:17; 92:4; 111:7, etc., etc.

Come, behold the works of the Lord.
—Old Testament: Psalms 46:8

"The works of the Lord" is so frequently repeated that only a few examples can be given.

I shall not die, but live, and declare the works of the Lord.
—Old Testament: Psalms 118:17

Great and marvellous are thy works, Lord God Almighty.
—New Testament: Revelation 15:3

The sun ariseth. . . . Man goeth forth unto his work and to his labor until the evening.
—Old Testament: Psalms 104:22–23

He gave . . . to every man his work.
—New Testament: Mark 13:34

The Lord shall deliver me from every evil work.
—New Testament: II Timothy 4:18

The Son of God was manifested, that he might destroy the works of the devil.
—New Testament: I John 3:8

He judgeth a man according to his works. . . . Every man shall find according to his works.
—Old Testament Apocrypha: Ecclesiasticus 16:12, 14

The Son of man . . . shall reward every man according to his works.
—New Testament: Matthew 16:27; II Timothy 4:14

The Father . . . judgeth according to every man's work.
—New Testament: I Peter 1:17

He that is unjust, let him be unjust still: and he which is filthy, let him be filthy still. . . . And, behold, I come quickly, . . . to give every man according as his work shall be.
—New Testament: Revelation 22:11–12

Commit thy works unto the Lord, and thy thoughts shall be established.
—Old Testament: Proverbs 16:3

There is nothing better, than that a man should rejoice in his own works; for that is his portion.
—Old Testament: Ecclesiastes 3:22

Then I beheld all the work of God, that a man cannot find out the work that is done under the sun: because though a man labor to seek it out, yet he shall not find it.
—Old Testament: Ecclesiastes 8:17

The Lord shall rise up, . . . that he may do his work, his strange work.
—Old Testament: Isaiah 28:21

I work a work in your days, a work which ye shall in no wise believe, though a man declare it unto you.
—New Testament: Acts 13:41

Then began he to upbraid the cities wherein most of his mighty works were done.
—New Testament: Matthew 11:20, 21, 23; Luke 10:13

The disciples began to rejoice and praise God with a loud voice for all the mighty works that they had seen.
—New Testament: Luke 19:37

Then said they unto him, What shall we do, that we might work the works of God? Jesus answered and said unto them, This is the work of God, that ye believe on him whom he hath sent.
—New Testament: John 6:28–29

I must work the works of him that sent me, while it is day: the night cometh, when no man can work.
—New Testament: John 9:4

The works that I do in my Father's name, they bear witness of me.
—New Testament: John 10:25

I have finished the work which thou gavest me to do.
—New Testament: John 17:4

God . . . hath saved us, . . . not according to our works, but according to his own purpose and grace.
—New Testament: II Timothy 1:8–9

Let every man prove his own work, and then shall he have rejoicing in himself alone, and not in another.
—New Testament: Galatians 6:4

Make you perfect in every good work.
—New Testament: Hebrews 13:21

The designation (HBBQ) indicates material taken from THE HOME BOOK OF BIBLE QUOTATIONS; (DB) signifies the DICTIONARY OF THE BIBLE; and (HBP) is THE HANDBOOK OF BIBLICAL PERSONALITIES.

He which hath begun a good work in you will perform it until the day of Jesus Christ.
> —New Testament: Philippians 1:6

Learn to maintain good works, . . . that they be not unfruitful.
> —New Testament: Titus 3:14

Let us consider one another to provoke unto love and to good works.
> —New Testament: Hebrews 10:24

By your good works . . . glorify God.
> —New Testament: I Peter 2:12
> (HBBQ)

WORLD–

The pillars of the earth are the Lord's, and he hath set the world upon them.
> —Old Testament: I Samuel 2:8

The world . . . he hath founded it upon the seas, and established it upon the floods.
> —Old Testament: Psalms 24:1–2

To the end of the world.
> —Old Testament: Psalms 19:4

And as he say upon the mount of Olives, the disciples came unto him privately, saying, Tell us, when shall these signs be? and what shall be the sign of thy coming, and of the end of the world?
> —New Testament: Matthew 24:3

Verses 3–31 are devoted to Jesus' enumeration of these signs.

Lo, I am with you alway, even unto the end of the world.
> —New Testament: Matthew 28:20

The world, and they that dwell therein [are the Lord's].
> —Old Testament: Psalms 24:1; 98:7; Nahum 1:5

Let all the inhabitants of the world stand in awe of him.
> —Old Testament: Psalms 33:8

All ye inhabitants of the world, . . . hear ye.
> —Old Testament: Isaiah 18:3

All the world wondered.
> —New Testament: Revelation 13:3

The world is mine, and the fulness thereof.
> —Old Testament: Psalms 50:12

Is this the man . . . That made the world as a wilderness, and destroyed the cities thereof?
> —Old Testament: Isaiah 14:16–17

Since the beginning of the world.
> —Old Testament: Isaiah 64:4;
> New Testament: Matthew 24:21;
> Acts 15:18; Ephesians 3:9

Since the world began.
> —New Testament: Luke 1:70; John 9:32;
> Acts 3:21; Romans 16:25

World without end.
> —Old Testament: Isaiah 45:17

He hath weighed the world in the balance.
> —Old Testament Apocrypha: II Esdras 4:36

The world is set in darkness, and they that dwell therein are without light.
> —Old Testament Apocrypha: II Esdras 14:20

Neither in this world, neither in the world to come.
> —New Testament: Matthew 12:32

He was in the world, and the world was made by him, and the world knew him not.
> —New Testament: John 1:10

Ye are of this world; I am not of this world.
> —New Testament: John 8:23

Marvel not, my brethren, if the world hate you.
> —New Testament: I John 3:13

The world by wisdom knew not God.
> —New Testament: I Corinthians 1:21

Know ye not that the friendship of the world is enmity with God? whosoever therefore will be a friend of the world is the enemy of God.
> —New Testament: James 4:4

Love not the world, neither the things that are in the world. If any man love the world, the love of the Father is not in him. For all that is in the world, the lust of the flesh, and the lust of th eeyes, and the pride of life, is not of the Father, but is of the world. And the world passeth away, and the lust thereof: but he that doeth the will of God abideth for ever.
> —New Testament: I John 2:15–17
> (HBBQ)

There is no single Hebrew word which can be translated *world*. When the visible universe is mentioned in a single phrase it is "heaven and earth"; but this phrase does not mean "world." The world (Greek *kosmos*) is conceived in Greek and modern thought as a systematic whole constituted by some unifying principle; in ancient

Semitic thought the "world was a sum of conflicting forces. The Greek word *kosmos* for world appears in the Old Testament only in late Greek books, and its use shows the influence of Greek usage. . . . *Kosmos* is also used to signify not the universe but the earth: man is created to manage the world. . . .

In the New Testament *kosmos* is both a cosmological and a theological term; it is far more common in the theological sense, but the two uses sometimes merge. God is the creator of the *kosmos;* it was made through the Word. The *kosmos* belongs to Christians (I Corinthians 3:22). The addition of "all in it" (Acts 17:24) echoes Hebrew "heaven and earth and all in them" and is Hebrew in thought rather than Greek; the *kosmos* is conceived as a spatial container, as it is in John 21:25. The *kosmos* is of limited duration: it has its age, its end and its beginning, which is its creation or its foundation. . . . The elements of the world which are served and which are in some sense hostile to God are obscure; some understand them as the Law, others as the elemental spirits which appear in Hellenistic syncretism. . . .

The world in a theological sense is the world as the scene of the process of salvation; it is not merely the scene but one of the protagonists of the drama, for the world is mankind as fallen, as alienated from God and hostile to God and to Jesus Christ. This conception is most frequent in the Pauline writings and in John, less frequent in the epistles and scarcely found at all in the Synoptic Gospels. The world stands in opposition to God; there is the spirit of the world and the spirit of God (I Corinthians 2:12). The wisdom, strength, and nobility of the world are the folly, weakness, and ignobility of God. The base of the opposition is found in the sinfulness of the world, the sin which entered the world through one man. . . . The world is hostile to God, but God is not hostile to the world. In Christ God reconciles the world to Himself. Christ came into the world to save sinners. But as long as the world remains unredeemed, Christians cannot identify themselves with it. . . .

In John the world becomes more prominent, and the opposition between God and Christ and the world is more sharply polarized. The purpose of God's salvation is the world and the mission of the Son is to it. He is the light of the world. John speaks frequently of the coming of Christ (the Son, the Word) into the world, this is never a simple coming, but has overtones of coming with a mission. Although Jesus comes into the world, He is not of the world (John 8:23). The world is loved by God so much that He sent His only son, and the mission of the Son is not to condemn but to save. He is the lamb who takes away the sin of the world, and the propitiation for the sins of the whole world.

But sinful humanity, to whom this mission of salvation comes, does not receive the mission nor the emissary; and it is in this aspect that the "world" in John becomes polarized into a kind of anti-God, a constant reality which is neither saved nor capable of salvation. The world recognizes and acknowledges neither Jesus nor the Father; indeed, the world hates Jesus. The world is under judgment, as is the ruler of the world, who has no power over Jesus. "The ruler of this world" is an obscure phrase which many interpreters understand to mean Satan, and this interpretation is possible. Other interpreters suggest that the ruler of this world is a collective personification of mankind unredeemed and hostile to God which sets itself up as an opposing power. The identification of Satan with the world as combined powers of evil is suggested in such verses as John 17:15; Jesus does not pray that the disciples be kept out of the world, but that the Father will protect them from the evil one. For the world Jesus does not pray; here certainly unredeemed humanity is conceived as a constant. The world can be redeemed and reconciled to God only by ceasing to be the world. The disciples, although they are men and live in the world as the universe and the scene of human life, do not belong to the world, as Jesus does not.

It is important to grasp the true meaning of "the world" in the New Testament in order that "unworldliness" may not be mere narrowness and intolerance, or mere external distinction from other men in manners and customs. Christians, like Jesus, are in the world and have a mission to the world and overcome it eventually by love and only by love.

(DB)

The designation (HBBQ) indicates material taken from THE HOME BOOK OF BIBLE QUOTATIONS; (DB) signifies the DICTIONARY OF THE BIBLE; and (HBP) is THE HANDBOOK OF BIBLICAL PERSONALITIES.

WORTHY–

I am not worthy of the least of all the mercies.
—Old Testament: Genesis 32:10

Whose shoes I am not worthy to bear.
—New Testament: Matthew 3:11

Lord, I am not worthy that thou shouldest come under my roof.
—New Testament: Matthew 8:8

He was not worthy of death.
—Old Testament: Deuteronomy 19:6

"Worthy of death" is repeated in Deuteronomy 21:22; I Kings 2:26.

They which commit such things are worthy of death.
—New Testament: Romans 1:32

I . . . am no more worthy to be called thy son.
—New Testament: Luke 15:19, 21

Who is worthy to open the book and to loose the seals thereof?
—New Testament: Revelation 5:2, 4
(HBBQ)

WRATH–

And it came to pass . . . that his wrath was kindled.
—Old Testament: Genesis 39:19

Great is the wrath of the Lord that is kindled against us.
—Old Testament: II Kings 22:13

Phrases frequently repeated.

Turn from thy fierce wrath, and repent of this evil against thy people.
—Old Testament: Exodus 32:12

I will pour out my wrath upon them like water.
—Old Testament: Hosea 5:10

While their meat was yet in their mouths, The wrath of God came upon them, and slew the fattest of them, and smote down the chosen men of Israel.
—Old Testament: Psalms 78:30–31

He that is slow to wrath is of great understanding.
—Old Testament: Proverbs 14:29

Let every man be swift to hear, slow to speak, slow to wrath. For the wrath of man worketh not the righteousness of God.
—New Testament: James 1:19–20

Jesus, which delivered us from the wrath to come.
—New Testament: I Thessalonians 1:10

All . . . when they heard these things, were filled with wrath.
—New Testament: Luke 4:28

Let not the sun go down upon your wrath.
—New Testament: Ephesians 4:26

Let all bitterness, and wrath, and anger, and clamour, and evil speaking, be put away from you, with all malice.
—New Testament: Ephesians 4:31;
Colossians 3:8

And the kings of the earth . . . said to the mountains and rocks, Fall on us, and hide us from the face of him that sitteth on the throne, . . . for the great day of his wrath is come.
—New Testament: Revelation 6:15–17

Pour out the vials of the wrath of God upon the earth.
—New Testament: Revelation 16:1

There were "seven golden vials full of the wrath of God," each containing a plague.

(HBBQ)

WRITING–

The Lord said unto Moses, . . . I will write upon these tables the words that were in the first tables.
—Old Testament: Exodus 34:1

Take thee a great roll, and write in it with a man's pen.
—Old Testament: Isaiah 8:1

It is a foolish thing to make a long prologue, and to be short in the story itself.
—Old Testament Apocrypha: II Maccabees 2:32
(HBBQ)

WRONG–

O Lord, thou hast seen my wrong: judge thou my cause.
—Old Testament: Lamentations 3:59

He suffered no man to do them wrong.
—Old Testament: I Chronicles 16:21;
Psalms 105:14

He that doeth wrong shall receive for the wrong which he hath done.
—New Testament: Colossians 3:25

Do no wrong . . . to the stranger, the fatherless, nor the widow.
—Old Testament: Jeremiah 22:3

We have wronged no man.
—New Testament: II Corinthians 7:2
(HBBQ)

· Y ·

YEAR–

A thousand years in thy sight are but as yesterday.
—Old Testament: Psalms 90:4

One day is with the Lord as a thousand years, and a thousand years as one day.
—New Testament: II Peter 3:8

We spend our years as a tale that is told.
—Old Testament: Psalms 90:9

This is the only use of "tale" in this sense in the Bible.

The days of our years are threescore years and ten.
—Old Testament: Psalms 90:10

The years of thy life shall be many. . . . The years of thy life shall be increased.
—Old Testament: Proverbs 4:10; 9:11

If a man live many years, and rejoice in them all; yet let him remember the days of darkness; for they shall be many.
—Old Testament: Ecclesiastes 11:8
(HBBQ)

YOKE–

Thou shalt break his yoke from off thy neck.
—Old Testament: Genesis 27:40

I was to them as they that take off the yoke on their jaws.
—Old Testament: Hosea 11:4

The yoke used by the Hebrews consisted of a short piece of wood, the bar, fitted with two pairs of converging pegs, the lower ends connected by thongs, the bands, to receive the necks of the draught animals.

It is good for a man that he bear the yoke in his youth. He sitteth alone and keepeth silence, because he hath borne it upon him.
—Old Testament: Lamentations 3:27–28

Take my yoke upon you, and learn of me; . . . For my yoke is easy, and my burden is light.
—New Testament: Matthew 11:29–30
(HBBQ)

YOUTH–

He was but a youth, and ruddy, and of a fair countenance.
—Old Testament: I Samuel 17:42

Young and tenderhearted.
—Old Testament: II Chronicles 13:7

The only use of "tenderhearted."

The glory of young men is their strength.
—Old Testament: Proverbs 20:29

Oh that I were . . . as I was in the days of my youth, when the secret of God was upon my tabernacle; When the Almighty was yet with me, when my children were about me; When I washed my steps with butter, and the rock poured me out rivers of oil; When I went out to the gate through the city, when I prepared my seat in the street!
—Old Testament: Job 29:2–7

Thy youth is renewed like the eagle's.
—Old Testament: Psalms 103:5

Rejoice, O young man, in thy youth; and let thy heart cheer thee in the days of thy youth, and walk in the ways of thine heart, and in the sight of thine eyes.
—Old Testament: Ecclesiastes 11:9

Thou hast not remembered the days of thy youth.
—Old Testament: Ezekiel 16:22, 43
(HBBQ)

The designation (HBBQ) indicates material taken from THE HOME BOOK OF BIBLE QUOTATIONS; (DB) signifies the DICTIONARY OF THE BIBLE; and (HBP) is THE HANDBOOK OF BIBLICAL PERSONALITIES.

· Z ·

ZACCHAEUS–

Jesus . . . passed through Jericho. And, behold, there was a man named Zacchaeus, which was the chief among the publicans, and he was rich. And he sought to see Jesus who he was; and could not for the press, because he was little of stature. And he ran before, and climbed up into a sycamore tree to see him.

—New Testament: Luke 19:1–4

One of the most famous jingles in the New England Primer describes this incident: "Zacchaeus he Did climb the tree His Lord to see."

And when Jesus came to the place, he looked up and saw him, and said unto him, Zacchaeus, make haste, and come down; for to day I must abide at thy house. And he made haste, and came down, and received him joyfully. And when they saw it, they all murmured, saying, That he was gone to be guest with a man that is a sinner. And Zacchaeus stood, and said unto the Lord; Behold, Lord, the half of my goods I give to the poor; and if I have taken any thing from any man by false accusation, I restore him fourfold. And Jesus said unto him, This day is salvation come to this house, forsomuch as he also is a son of Abraham.

—New Testament: Luke 19:5–9

The only use of "forsomuch." "Fourfold" is used once again in II Samuel 12:6. A publican was a tax collector, not the keeper of a "pub," as now commonly used; and Hebrews who collected taxes for the Romans were detested by their co-religionists as traitors. These collectors habitually extorted excessive taxes, hence Zacchæus's promise to restore fourfold whatever he had taken by false accusation.

(HBBQ)

ZADOK—Just, Righteous.

Zadok was one of several prominent priests in Jerusalem in the time of David. Abiathar was another, as was his son Ahimelech. In the rebellion of Absalom, when David was forced out of his city, Zadok and Abiathar, together with their sons, were instructed to remain in Jerusalem to guard the ark and to act as informers for the king. Here it appears that Zadok and Abiathar were priests of equal status in the court, although II Samuel 8:17 states that "Zadok . . . and Ahimelech the son of Abiathar were priests. . . ."
In the attempt of Adonijah to take the throne in David's latter days, Zadok took the side of Solomon, Abiathar the side of Adonijah. When Nathan the prophet and Bathsheba prevailed on David to declare Solomon king and to have him crowned at once, it was Zadok who anointed Solomon and placed the crown on his head. The king then made Zadok chief priest and banished Abiathar to his home in Anathoth.
Zadok and his family became the first family of the priesthood in Jerusalem. When, under Josiah in 621 B.C., worship was centralized in the city, the "Zadokites," priests of the family of Zadok, were among the most influential people in all Israel. The position of the family was, of course, contested by other priestly families; but Ezekiel supports the Zadokites as having exclusive rights to the priestly office. Ezekiel was himself a priest of the line of Zadok. The Chronicler took care to trace Zadok to the elder of Aaron's sons and so to enhance the already secure position of his descendants.

(HBP)

ZEALOTS–

In New Testament times the Zealots were a Jewish sect which represented the extreme of fanatic nationalism. Their belief in the messianism of the Old Testament was entirely limited to the recovery of Jewish independence; they believed in the worship of Yahweh alone and were convinced that acceptance of foreign domination and payment of taxes to a foreign ruler was a blasphemy against Yahweh. The party seems to have originated in the revolt against the census taken under Quirinius. The sect was a minority and was regarded by other Jews with distaste at least. Their tactics were those of the modern political terrorists; they raided and killed frequently, attacking both foreigners and Jews whom they suspected of what is more recently called "collaboration." They carried the art of assassination to such a point of skill that the Romans called them *sicarii* ("stabbers") from their practice of concealing a dagger beneath the garments for stealthy use in crowded areas. Their largest concerted effort before the outbreak of the Jewish war was a raid of reprisal on Samaria for an assault on Jewish pilgrims under the procurator Ventidius Cumanus (48–52). Their fanaticism and their tactics are illustrated in the life of Paul, who was threatened with assassination by a group of men (Acts 23:12–15). One of the disciples of Jesus, Simon, was called the Zealot; he was probably a former member of the sect. They were chiefly responsible for the outbreak of the rebellion against Rome in 66, and forced the moderates to accept the rebellion even against their will; and during the next few years they obtained control of Jerusalem by the suppression or murder of those who opposed their extreme policies. They maintained pockets of resistance in the country after the fall of Jerusalem, and the movement survived long enough to break out again in the rebellion of 132–135 under Hadrian.

(DB)

ZEBULUN–Dwelling.

Genesis 30:20; 35:23; 46:14; 49:13; Judges 1:30; 4:6, 10; 5:14, 18; 6:35; 12:12; etc.
The sixth son of Jacob by Leah, his tenth son. Three of the clans of nomads stem from Zebulun's sons—Sered, Elon and Jahleel. Judges 5, the Song of Deborah, counts the Zebulunites as among those responding to the call to arms. The wording of the song indicates that Zebulun contributed leadership to the cause, for they were said to "bear the marshal's staff."

(HBP)

ZECHARIAH–

1. St. Luke 1:5 f.; 3:2.
The father of John the Baptist. Zechariah was a priest in the Temple at Jerusalem. He and his wife Elizabeth were "righteous before God" and "blameless," but they had no child and they were well along in years.
As he performed his duties of burning incense while the people were at prayer, an angel appeared to be standing before him on the right side of the altar of incense. The angel, Gabriel, calmed his fear and gave him the promise of a son, to be called John, a son who would be called also "great" because he would be "in the spirit of Elijah," and would prepare the way for the Messiah.

Zechariah was dubious and expressed his doubts. Gabriel then said that for his doubt he would be unable to speak until all the promised things concerning John were fulfilled. When John was born the question of naming him was debated within the family. Elizabeth said he should be named John and her statement was confirmed by Zechariah who, still speechless, wrote the name on a tablet. When he had finished the writing, his "tongue was loosed," and he praised God with the words now known and used as the *Benedictus,* a much loved canticle in the liturgy of the Church.
2. II Kings 14:29; 15:8–11.
The son of Jeroboam II, Zechariah was king of Israel for six months, c. 746–745 B.C. He was killed by Shallum the son of Jabesh, who held the throne for one month.
3. II Chronicles 24:20–22; St. Matthew 23:35; St. Luke 11:51.
Zechariah was the son of the faithful priest, Jehoiada, who had helped save young Joah from the murderous wrath of his grandmother and later had helped bring him to the throne. During Jehoiada's lifetime the old priest was a trusted and honored advisor to King Joash. When he died, however, the king turned to counselors who led him away from the policies of Jehoiada, and the people "forsook the house of the Lord," with the result that "wrath came upon Judah and Jerusalem."
At this point Zechariah "stood above the people" and rebuked them for their sins, saying, "Because you have forsaken the Lord, he has forsaken you." The people "conspired" against him and at the king's command they stoned him to death. As he died, Zechariah said, "May the Lord see and avenge!"
The gospels of Matthew and Luke refer to the death of Zechariah, obviously the same man although called the son of Barachiah, as having been "murdered between the sanctuary and the altar."
4. II Kings 18:2; II Chronicles 29:1.
The father of Abi (Abijah), who was the wife of Ahaz and mother of Hezekiah, kings of Judah.
5. Ezra 5:1; 6:14; Zechariah 1:1; 7:1, 8.
Zechariah, the son of Berechiah, son of Iddo, was a prophet in Judah. His activities as a prophet may be dated as contemporaneous with the latter part

of the work of Haggai, *c.* 520 B.C. and following.

Although Zechariah was much concerned to call the people to repentance, he intimated that repentance had been shown and that the purpose of the Lord in chastising the people had been accomplished. "As the Lord of hosts purposed to deal with us for our ways and deeds, so he has dealt with us." And that being so, the angel of the Lord said to Zechariah, "I have returned to Jerusalem with compassion; my house shall be built in it. . . ." Thus the "four horns" of Zechariah's vision, horns which had been used to scatter Israel, were now to be used to put down the nations which had done more than enough of the purpose of the Lord. The line in the hands of the "man" met by the prophet was a "measuring line" to be used in measuring Jerusalem for rebuilding. The call of the Lord was heard as "Ho! Escape to Zion, you who dwell with the daughter of Babylon."

Zechariah envisioned in Zerubbabel, called Joshua in chapter 3, the Messiah, who "Not by might, nor by power, but by my spirit" would rule the land and the people in the name of the Lord. Stealing and the bearing of false witness in the new kingdom would be so punished as to come to an end. Wickedness would be "thrust down" and borne away to the "land of Shinar." Zerubbabel who had laid the foundations of the new Temple would see it completed, and in the new regime the remnant of Israel would be prosperous and at peace—no longer a curse, but a blessing. The peoples of the nations would want to go with the Jews to their city to worship their God; for, they would say, "We have heard that God is with you."

The coronation of Zerubbabel, of course, failed to materialize. The Persian officers got wind of it, and Zerubbabel disappeared.

The prophet shows many similarities to Ezekiel, and a strength of hope in sharp contrast to the dour thoughts of many another prophet.

The Book of Zechariah, however, contains materials much later than those of the prophet himself. Chapter 9–14 consist of two "Oracles" from the Greek rather than the Persian period (9:13, e.g.). From these chapters several thoughts and phrases have been taken much to heart by Christians. For example, the story of the Triumphal Entry of Jesus into Jerusalem is phrased in words from Zechariah 9:9 (St. Matthew 21:5); the thirty pieces of silver as the price of betrayal (St. Matthew 27:9 f.) may be found in Zechariah 11:12 f.; the words of Jesus in St. Mark 14:27 ("I will stroke the shepherd, and the sheep will be scattered") are a quotation from Zechariah 13:7; and the words in St. John 19:37, "They shall look on him whom they have pierced," are from Zechariah 12:10.

As chapters 1–8 reveal the influence of Ezekiel in many ways, so do chapters 9–14 show clearly the characteristics of the later apocalyptic style.

(HBP)

ZEDEKIAH–Yahweh is Might.
1. I Kings 22:11, 24; II Chronicles 18:10, 23.
A false prophet who, using a pair of horns to symbolize his words, told Ahab and Jehoshaphat that if they went to battle against the Syrians at Ramoth-gilead they would be victorious. With his horns of iron before him, Zedekiah said, "With these you shall push the Syrians until they are destroyed." Jehoshaphat was suspicious of the prophecy, however, and Micaiah was called to give an oracle. When Micaiah spoke favorable words, Ahab was suspicious, and finally Micaiah told him the truth as he saw it; namely, that the Lord had said, "Who will entice Ahab, that he may go up and fall at Ramoth-gilead?" In the conflict of prophecies in which Zedekiah was in effect called a liar by Micaiah, Zedekiah "struck Micaiah on the cheek."
2. II Kings 24:17–25:7; I Chronicles 3:15; II Chronicles 36:10; Jeremiah 1:3; 21:1–14; 24:28–10; 27:1–28:1; 29:3; 32:1–5; 34:2 f.; 37:1 f.; 38:5–39:10; 44:30; 49:34; 51:59; 52:1–11.
The youngest son of Josiah who was appointed king of Judah under Nebuchadnezzar, 597 B.C. Originally his name was Mattaniah. The king of Babylon seems to have been involved in the change of names as well as in the appointment. Zedekiah took an oath of obedience to Babylon, but he joined a coalition of Moab, Ammon, and Tyre against Nebuchadnezzar after considerable hesitation and vascillation. In 588 B.C. there was open revolt. Egypt promised assistance, an important factor in the decision to rebel. Babylon laid siege to Jerusalem, but the siege was lifted when word came that Egypt's chariots were coming up. Jeremiah, who had urged submission to Babylon,

was thrown into a cistern; but even from the cistern he contended that salvation for the city depended upon submission. Babylon renewed the attack and took Jerusalem in 586 B.C. Zedekiah tried to escape but was captured and taken to Babylon where he was forced to watch the slaying of his sons, and then was himself blinded. He remained a captive in Babylon.

3. Jeremiah 29:21 f.

A prophet in the time of Jeremiah who, because he aroused hopes for delivery of the city of Jerusalem from the Babylonian threat, was strongly opposed by Jeremiah. Zedekiah's prophecies played a part in the revolt against Nebuchadnezzar, which brought about the disastrous siege of Jerusalem and its final fall in 586 B.C. Jeremiah accused Zedekiah of immorality as well as false prophecies. For his part in stimulating the revolt Nebuchadnezzar put Zedekiah to torture by having him roasted in a fire.

(HBP)

ZEPHANIAH–Yahweh is Darkness.

1. The Book of Zephaniah.

During the reign of Josiah, the prophet Zephaniah spoke of judgment to come upon his people, and and on all the peoples of the earth, because of the idolatry and immorality prevalent amongst them. The word of the Lord to him was that the earth would be "devoured with the fire of my jealousy," but afterward the "remnant in Israel," and through them other peoples, would turn "to a pure language." He said that the God of Israel, standing in the midst of the purified peoples, would hear their shouts of joy and praise and thanksgiving. Israel, after the holocaust, would be a "name and a praise among all the peoples of the earth."

Zephaniah, the son of Cushi, claimed royal ancestry through Hezekiah. Since many of the things condemned in his prophecies were changed to some degree by the reforms of Josiah in 621 B.C., it might be supposed that Zephaniah prophesied somewhat before that date.

2. II Kings 25:18; Jeremiah 21:1; 29:25 f.; 37:3; 52:24 f.

Zephaniah was "second priest," i.e. next to the chief priest, in Jerusalem at the time of the fall of the city to Nebuchadnezzar. He stood with King Zedekiah against the idea of Jeremiah that the city should submit to the Chaldeans. He was employed by the king to confer with Jeremiah in an effort to silence him or to persuade him to change his opinions. Jeremiah was adamant, both in his opinion as to the need to work with the Babylonians and also in his attitude as to the length of the exile.

Zephaniah, with many others, was taken to Riblah by the captain of the Chaldean guard. There they were taken to the king who had them executed.

(HBP)

ZERUBBABEL–Offspring, or Shoot of Babylon.

1 Chronicles 3:19; Ezra 2:2; 3:2 f.; 4:2 f.; 5:2; Nehemiah 7:7; 12:1, 47; Haggai 1:1, 12 f.; 2:2 f.; Zechariah 4:6 f.

The governor of Judah who was chosen as one of the group to return from exile and to rebuild the Temple in Jerusalem, by permission of Darius. He was largely responsible for the task and actually accomplished it, although he was forced by his opponents, first Rehum the commander and Shimshai the scribe, then Tattenai the governor, to appeal to the king for help. Zerubbabel was much respected and beloved by his associates, who regarded him somewhat as a saviour. Zechariah seems to have wanted him crowned as the Messiah. As the Book of Haggai closes, the prophet says: "In that day, says the Lord of hosts, I will take you, O Zerubbabel my servant, the son of Shealtiel, says the Lord, and may you like a signet ring; for I have chosen you, says the Lord of hosts."

(HBP)

ZIBA–Strength(?) Crier, Yelper(?)

II Samuel 9:1–12; 16:1–4; 19:17 f.

One of Saul's household, possibly a slave at the time of Saul's death, who became wealthy and influential, and a counselor to King David. He informed David of the condition of the remaining members of Saul's family after David rose to power, and it was through Ziba that David was enabled to show kindness to Mephibosheth, Jonathan's crippled son. The king made Ziba the steward of all the lands to which Mephibosheth was entitled.

Later, as David fled Jerusalem in the uprising of

The designation (HBBQ) indicates material taken from THE HOME BOOK OF BIBLE QUOTATIONS; (DB) signifies the DICTIONARY OF THE BIBLE; and (HBP) is THE HANDBOOK OF BIBLICAL PERSONALITIES.

Absalom, he met Ziba as he brought provisions for the retinue of the king. On inquiring for Mephibosheth he was told, slyly, that Jonathan's son stayed on in the city with the notion that now the kingdom would be returned to Saul's house. David then gave Ziba all Mephibosheth's possessions; but after Mephibosheth gave a good account of his actions caused by his lameness, half of his inheritance was returned to him. Ziba, former servant or slave in a king's house, thus became lord of half the dead king's private fortunes.

(HBP)

ZION–

> Zion, which is the city of David.
> —Old Testament: I Chronicles 11:5

According to the majority of modern scholars, Zion was situated on the hill known as Ophel, the south-eastern of the four hills of Jerusalem. The "city of David" because he fixed on Jerusalem as his capital when he became king of Israel, and founded the royal city on Mount Zion. See II Samuel 5:7.

> God will save Zion, and will build the cities of Judah.
> —Old Testament: Psalms 69:35

> They that trust in the Lord shall be as mount Zion, which cannot be removed, but abideth for ever.
> —Old Testament: Psalms 125:1

> Out of Zion shall go forth the law.
> —Old Testament: Isaiah 2:3; Micah 4:2

> O Zion, that bringest good tidings, get thee up into the high mountain.
> —Old Testament: Isaiah 40:9

> Arise ye, and let us go up to Zion unto the Lord our God.
> —Old Testament: Jeremiah 31:6

> Zion spreadeth forth her hands, and there is none to comfort her.
> —Old Testament: Lamentations 1:17

> Be glad then, ye children of Zion, and rejoice.
> —Old Testament: Joel 2:23

> Saith the Lord, I am returned unto Zion, and will dwell in the midst of Jerusalem.
> —Old Testament: Zechariah 8:3
> (HBBQ)

ZIPPORAH–Little Bird.

Exodus 2:21; 4:25; 18:2

The daughter of Jethro, the priest of Midian. Zipporah became Moses' wife. Gershom and Eliezer were her sons. Moses "sent her away" from Egypt, and with her sons she returned to her father in Midian. In Exodus 4:24–26 there is an interesting story probably intending to account for the origin of circumcising infants instead of waiting, as in former times, until young men reached the age of puberty or until a time just before marriage. Moses had not been circumcised. He became ill and Zipporah thought this deficiency the cause of his illness. She circumcised her young son with a "flint" and touched Moses' "feet" to make the rite count for him as well as for her son. This, as the story suggests, corrected the fault in Moses and saved his life.

(HBP)

INDEX

Objects and Monuments

Reproductions

Epistles

24. E. Presuhn: *La piu belle pareti di Pompei.* Torino, 1877, Pl. LV
27. A. B. Cook: *Zeus.* Cambridge, 1914, Frontispiece
29. Drawing of crowns—*Ephemeris Archaiologike,* 1862, No. 219, Pl. 34
32. S. Reinach: *Repertoire de peintures grecques et romaines.* Paris, 1922, p. 239 (3)
35. Musil: *Kuseir Amra.* Wien, 1907, Pls. XL, XLI
53. Above—F. Cabrol—H. Leclercq: *Dictionarie d'arch-éologie chretienne,* VI. Paris, 1925, Fig. 1553, Coll. 887–888
    Below—O. Jahn in *Berichte sachs. Ges. Wissensch.* 1861, Pl. X, 6
56. M. Rostovtzeff—F. Brown, ed.: *Excavations at Dura Europos,* Provisional Report, V, 1934, Pls. XXXIX, XLVIII
58. *Wiener Genesis,* ed. H. Gertsinger, Wien, 1931, Pl. 7
55. Reconstructed drawing—O. Bender: *Roma, 1910,* P. 200

Revelation

75. Drawing—Th. Schrieber: *Kulturhistorischer Bilder-atlas,* Leipzig, 1888. Pl. XV
89. A. Deissman: Light from the Ancient East. London, 1907, Fig. 62, opp. p. 341
99. Vigoroux: *Dictionnaire biblique II.* Paris, 1910, Fig. 578, Col. 1819

Photographs

Epistles

The Orient Press Photo Company: 17, 59, 67
E. Nash, Rome: 20
Placed at the disposal of the Editor: 19, 43, 44

Revelation

The Orient Press Photo Company: 78, 92
Placed at the disposal of the Editor: 74

Creative Kids

Art for All Seasons

Written by Susie Alexander

Teacher Created Materials, Inc.

Teacher Created Materials, Inc.
6421 Industry Way
Westminster, CA 92683
Teacher Created Materials, Inc.
© 2004
Made in U.S.A.
ISBN-0-7439-3198-x

Editor:
Janet Cain
Cover Artist:
Brenda DiAntonis
Illustrator:
Wendy Chang

The materials in this book may be reproduced for personal or classroom use only. The reproduction of any part of this publication for an entire school or school system is strictly prohibited.

No part of this publication may be transmitted, stored, or recorded in any form without permission from the publisher.